NATURE, PROPERTIES, AND LAWS OF WEALTH

Beginning of a New Science

B. V. Gopinath

University Press of America,® Inc.
Lanham · Boulder · New York · Toronto · Plymouth, UK

Copyright © 2009 by
University Press of America,® Inc.
4501 Forbes Boulevard
Suite 200
Lanham, Maryland 20706
UPA Acquisitions Department (301) 459-3366

Estover Road
Plymouth PL6 7PY
United Kingdom

Library of Congress Control Number: 2008934818
ISBN-13: 978-0-7618-4363-4 (paperback : alk. paper)
ISBN-10: 0-7618-4363-9 (paperback : alk. paper)
eISBN-13: 978-0-7618-4364-1
eISBN-10: 0-7618-4364-7

The Book is dedicated to my beloved Professor,
DR. T. SHESHAGIRI RAO,
M. Sc Agriculture, Ph.D.
Retired Professor and Head,
Department of Chemistry and Soils,
College of Agriculture,
Dharwad,
Karnataka, India.

CONTENTS

Preface

Some similarities appear accidental but deeper learning tells us a different story. I am referring here to the similarity between chemistry and economics. Former is a study of nature, composition, properties, laws and classification of matter and the latter, though defined differently, is a study of nature, composition, properties, laws, and classification of wealth. The laws governing matter, energy and wealth are same: the Law of Conservation and Law of Equilibrium. No attempt was made by any one in the past to study wealth the way chemists studied matter. This book is an attempt in this direction to unearth the general properties and general laws of wealth so as to simplify study of wealth.

Economics studied application of wealth in greater detail and hence was rightly classified as social science. But my honest opinion is that there should be a science in place to study nature, composition, properties, laws and classification of wealth. Economists may not like to change their course of study and hence it is my appeal that a new science with specific subject matter dealing with wealth be named and studied in all earnest. This science, being a replica of chemistry, needs to be studied by students of material or physical science. As this science unveils one finds this to be a mirror image of chemistry. This science has foolproof answers to many questions that people have found hard to answer.

Law of Conservation and Law of Equilibrium are two important laws that have given birth to several laws and theories in chemistry, physics, biology and economics. An offshoot of these laws, the Law of Mass Action of chemical reactions amply explains every phenomenon in economics. Like matter and energy, wealth also moves from higher concentration to lower concentration.

Matter, energy, wealth and soul are the manifestations of the God. One can neither create nor destroy matter/energy/wealth/soul/God. Matter, energy, wealth and soul are inter-convertble. All studies lead us to Him. The ultimate aim of this study is to have better understanding of His creations and His Laws.

This study of nature, properties, composition, laws and classification of wealth, (We may call this chemistry of wealth) has applications in every field. This science is useful in making policy decisions, in preparing fiscal budget and monetary policy, in understanding accounting procedures and to evolve scientific taxation.

Gulbarga   B.V. Gopinath
Karnataka   December 2007
India

CHAPTER I
INTRODUCTION

Wealth is a subject of importance to every one. Every one is supposed to know basics of the nature, properties, laws and classification of wealth. Wealth, like matter and energy has some important general properties. There are some important general laws relating to every form of wealth. Though the laws and properties of wealth are distinctly visible, efforts are not made to study them in a systematic way. The application of this study is in every field, be it in economics, be it in accountancy, be it in policy making, be it business management, be it in budgeting household expenditure, be it in running an organization or association.

Ignorance is at large in understanding the nature, properties, laws and classification of wealth. There are confusions in the minds of the people as to what constitutes wealth. This is evident from various definitions of wealth one reads in web pages. People say time is precious. Is time a form of wealth? Economists use the term marginal utility. Is Utility a form of wealth? Accountants use terms like depreciation, loss, goodwill, expenditure etc. Are they forms of wealth? Are all items shown in financial statements forms of wealth? In the process of photosynthesis, soil moisture, essential plant nutrients present in the soil, chlorophyll, carbon dioxide and sunlight jointly manufacture food. Are they all forms of wealth? If one goes by the definition of wealth of economists, wealth is one that has value in use and value in exchange. If so, chlorophyll, carbon dioxide, loss depreciation, goodwill, etc., that may/may not have "Value in exchange", are not forms of wealth. Can there be a foolproof definition of wealth that is appropriate for all. Can labor and wages be classified in same kind of wealth? How far human behavior influences the properties of wealth? What role social factors play in this study?

This study (that deals with nature, properties, laws and classification of wealth) has no name as on date. One cannot call it economics. The definition of economics as stated by economist Alfred Marshall in his book principles of economics is "Economics is a study of mankind in the ordinary business of life. Does this mean study of nature, properties, laws and classification of wealth? Economics is subdivided into branches like econometrics, macroeconomics, microeconomics, quantitative economics, history of economic thought, environmental economics, international economics, labor economics, behavioral economics etc.

Where does this study of wealth, fit into? This is not a social science by any stretch of imagination. This study is a mirror image of chemistry. This subject embodies principles of economics, principles of double entry bookkeeping, some aspects of financial management and business management.

The great economist Adam Smith, in his book Wealth of the Nations, defines economics as science of wealth. Where did the economists err? Economists concentrated on application of wealth rather than knowing nature, properties, composition and laws of wealth. This led them to the path of social sciences because the application of wealth is related to social aspects. Had there been an attempt to know wealth, its nature, general properties and laws, they would have certainly classified economics as a material or physical science. Perhaps this is a human tendency. People hesitate to call themselves scientists of fundamental or basic sciences. They prefer the words applied, advanced, technical, super-specialized, hi-tech etc rather than fundamental or basic. This is the reason why basic and general properties and laws of wealth are neglected. We forget to analyze things that are right before us. Had mankind given due importance to cultivation of grasses the problems of soil erosion, depletion of ground water resources, silting of tanks and reservoirs etc would have been unheard of. It is again true that mankind neglected omnipresent grass and cared little for this useful living substance. Without improving fundamental physical properties of soils we cannot achieve soil and water conservation. There is not a single laboratory in India to test the physical properties of soils of farmers' fields. This amply proves how much we care for fundamental or basic aspects. I am sorry that the soil scientist in me wrote these lines, which are not relevant to study of wealth. It must be remembered that without sound fundamental knowledge solutions to problems are hard to come by.

The methodology adopted here is the one adopted by chemists in studying nature, properties, laws and classification of matter. The material scientists first explore possibility of common properties and common laws in existence. They then proceed with sub-classification grouping forms of wealth with some common properties. There are some common laws for matter, energy and wealth. Law of Conservation and Law of Dynamic Equilibrium are the two important laws that determine the properties of matter and wealth. Law of Mass Action of chemistry is an important Law that applies to all economic reactions where wealth changes from one form to another. All economic reactions are reversible in nature i.e. wealth changes from reactant to product and product to reactant forms. Thus one should have noticed that in double entry bookkeeping, there is a credit entry of like amount for every debit entry.

This science is a mirror image of chemistry. Principle of equivalent weight of chemistry is not new to economists. Price is one name for equivalent weight.

In chemistry one form of matter reacts with another form of matter in the ratio of equivalent weight. We observe in economic reactions, say sale, one form of wealth reacts (or gets exchanged for), with another form of wealth in the ratio of price. The formulae used in chemistry: $N_1V_1 = N_2V_2$ is also applicable to various economic reactions. Water is described as Universal Solvent in chemistry. So is Utility of economics. All forms of wealth are soluble in this form of wealth called Utility. The concepts of solubility of physical chemistry are very useful in this study. These concepts would amply explain why an obsolete car exits the market. These concepts also explain the strategy to be adopted to overcome the competition and retain solubility of the products in the form of wealth called "Utility." Chemists use some techniques to speed up chemical reactions. These techniques are applicable to economic reactions as well and one would say that they are very handy for speeding up economic reaction like "*Sale.*"

This is a new science or one would say that an existing science studied with different tools. The scope of this study is vast. The applications are omnipresent. A beginning is made. It needs patronage from educationalists to grow.

CHAPTER II
DEFINITION OF WEALTH

It is interesting to know what people think about wealth. The definitions of wealth, as one finds in various web pages speak of varied concepts people hold about wealth. To narrate, I quote a few below (Source: www.google.com. define: wealth)

1. The state of being rich and affluent; having plentiful supply of material goods and money; "great wealth is not a great sign of intelligence.
2. The quality of profuse abundance: "she has a wealth of talent."
3. An abundance of material possessions and resources.
4. Property that has economic utility; a monetary value or an exchange value wordnet.princeton.edu/perl/webwn
5. The value of one's total possessions and property rights.
   www.ncbuy.com/credit/glossary.html
6. Total assets minus total liabilities.
   www.econplace.com/mm5e/glossary.html
7. The total value of the accumulated assets owned by an individual, household, community or country.
   www-personal.umich.edu/~alandear/glossary/w.html
8 The things that create happiness. Many, but not all, are things that can be bought with money. (Important note: Money is not wealth: the stuff money buys is wealth).
   Web2.airmail.net/scsr/Define5.htm
9. The value of all the things that people own.
   www.econ100.com/eu5e/open/glossary.html
10. The net gain in material well-being from an economic activity. Wealth is measured according to the items of value in a given culture.
   Orgonstate.edu./instruct/anth370/gloss/html

All the above definitions of wealth spoke of a few characteristics of wealth. No definition described wealth in total. What is wealth then? Matter, wealth, energy and soul are the God's creations. OR The God Almighty manifests himself in these four forms. All are inter-dependent and all have something in common.

The great economist, Adam Smith defined economics as science of wealth. Unfortunately economists concentrated on application or use of wealth and neglected the nature, properties, laws and classification of wealth. In any book on economics, one finds the description of wealth. One also finds the properties of wealth described that mainly pertain to use of wealth. Wealth is said to be one that has "Value in Use" and "Value in Exchange." This emphasis on value in exchange is a result of direction of study of wealth from application angle. Economists also say that wealth is one that is scarce. Commodities like carbon dioxide, sunlight, chlorophyll, essential plant nutrients present in the soil, oxygen etc., that have Value in Use are not treated as wealth as they do not have "Value in Exchange." These commodities are not scarce either. Water, when abundant, loses to be a wealth and when it becomes scarce, it acquires the property of wealth. When a commodity that has Value in Use is changed to a commodity that has Value in Exchange, it is generally conceived as creation of wealth. Similarly, when a commodity that has Value in Exchange is changed to a commodity that has Value in Use, the same is construed as destruction of wealth. In economics, we have a principle that Income = Expenditure + Savings. All expenditure that one incurs may or may not have Value in Exchange. Is expenditure a form of wealth?

Accountancy is about study of sources and application of wealth. Wealth is measured and appropriated in different heads of accounts. As a beginner, one can think that all that are shown in financial statements are forms of wealth. There is no authentic definition of wealth by accountants on record. One can presume that all that are shown in financial statements are construed as wealth. Items like depreciation, loss, goodwill and items of expenditure that may/may not have Value in Exchange are shown in financial statements. Are they forms of wealth?

In economics, in the first chapter of any book, one reads that man has wants. To fulfill his wants he has at his disposal means. Are means and wants forms of wealth? The demand and supply are the common terms one hears daily. Are they forms of wealth?

There are units of measurement in place for measuring matter and energy. What are the units of measurement of non-wealth? Can the units of wealth be applied to measure non-wealth? One does not find in any book any mention about units of non-wealth. Therefore all that are measurable and all that have units of measurement are wealth. If one considers Value in Use as the qualifying condition for consideration as form of wealth, all that the God has created has Value in Use in one way or the other. Even the harmful bacteria and carnivorous animals are of ecological importance. For an environmental economist they are wealth.

If one goes by the doctrine of mathematics, 2a can be added to 5a and the result is 7a. 2a can be subtracted from 5a and the result is 3a. Can one add 2a and 3b? No, unless "a" and "b" are inter-convertible. Can one subtract 2a from

7b? No, unless "a" and "b" are inter-convertible. Can one add 2kg and 5kg? Yes. Can one subtract 2kg from 5kg? Yes. Can one add 3kg and 5m? No. Similarly one cannot subtract 5kg from 7m. Let "a" be wealth and "b" be non-wealth. They cannot be added or subtracted to/from one another. The inference one draws from this is that *Only Wealth Can Be Added/Subtracted To/From Wealth*. This leads us to first general law of wealth called *Law Of Conservation Of Wealth*. As wealth only can be added to/subtracted from wealth, wealth can neither be created nor be destroyed but can be changed from one form to

another. This Law is common to matter and energy as well. Coming to items like loss, goodwill, expenditure and depreciation that may or may not have Value in Exchange, one finds that these are expressed in units of known form of wealth i.e. money and these are added to or subtracted from other forms of wealth. Hence they are forms of wealth even though they may not have Value in Exchange. In the following example:

Sun light + Soil moisture + carbon dioxide + essential plant nutrients → food (In presence of chlorophyll), one finds that items like sunlight, carbon dioxide, soil moisture and essential plant nutrients that have no Value in Exchange combine to form food, a form of wealth that has Value in Exchange. According to doctrine of mathematics, sunlight, soil moisture, carbon dioxide and essential plant nutrients present in the soil are all forms of wealth. Therefore, the natural consequence of the discussion presented here would suffice to show that wealth may/may not necessarily have Value in Exchange.

From above discussions, we may conclude that wealth is one that is measurable (in units), one that has value-in-use, wealth is one that can be added to or subtracted from other forms of wealth and one that can be changed to other forms of wealth. I remember the most comprehensive definition of agriculture stated by Dr. F.E. Allison in his book "Soil organic matter and its role in crop production." Dr. Allison wrote, "Agriculture is all about utilization of solar energy for fulfillment of human needs." A definition should be comprehensive and general.

I summarize: one that is measurable and one that has value in use is wealth. Wealth, as revealed in the chapter "Movement and wealth and Law of Equilibrium," always moves from higher concentration to lower concentration till equilibrium is reached.

CHAPTER III

LAW OF CONSERVATION OF WEALTH

Laws of wealth amply speak of properties of wealth. Properties and laws are inter-dependent. There are two laws applicable to all forms of wealth in general. These laws apply to matter and energy as well. The two laws are Law of Conservation of Wealth and Law of Equilibrium. If one is a believer of Bhagavad-Gita, one believes that Law of Conservation applies to soul as well. Law of Conservation applies to all creations of the God (matter, soul, energy and wealth) and one may say that this law is a manifestation of the God. There can be no science without these two laws. Their presence is visible in mathematics, chemistry, physics, biology, economics, accountancy, business management, philosophy, psychology and any other subject one may think of. These two laws are co-existent and one does not operate in isolation of the other. Law of Conservation is the cause and Law of Equilibrium is the effect. The application of these two laws is so vast that no one can completely describe their importance even if one spends one's entire life in describing the importance. All other laws and theories are derived from these two laws. My contribution here may be treated as my mark of respect to these universal laws made by the God Almighty.

One should study Law of Conservation of Mass and Law of Conservation of Energy to understand Law of Conservation of Wealth. Law of Conservation of Mass applies to matter and Law of Conservation of Energy applies to energy. Both these Laws are stated in similar words. It is natural that Law of Conservation of Wealth can be stated on similar lines.

Law of Conservation of Mass:

When matter changes from one form to the other, there will be no change in the mass. The mass of transferee form of matter equals mass of transferor form of matter. This leads to inference that matter can neither be created nor be destroyed but can be changed from one form to another. Let us understand the concept with some examples. When ice melts into water, mass of ice equals mass of water. This is an example of physical change. Let us consider an example of chemical change. 80grams of sodium hydroxide reacts with 98 grams of sulfuric acid to form 142 grams of sodium sulfate and 36 gram of water. One would see that the total mass of reactants- sodium hydroxide and sulfuric acid equals total mass of products- sodium sulfate and water. Mass of reactants = mass of products.

Law of Conservation of Energy:

In any process involving transfer of energy from one form to the other, total quantity of energy in the form of transferor form equals total quantity of energy in the transferee form. This leads to inference that energy can neither be created nor be destroyed but can be changed from one form to the other.

Law of Conservation of Wealth:

Law of Conservation of wealth can be stated on similar lines. When wealth changes from one form to another, the value of wealth of transferor form equals value of wealth of transferee form. This leads to an important inference that wealth can neither be created nor be destroyed but can be changed from one form to another.

In our daily life, we come across several cases where wealth changes form one form to the other. When one buys a commodity, in his hands, wealth in the form of cash gets changed to wealth in the form of commodity. In the hands of the seller, a reverse change takes place. Commodity, a form of wealth, changes into money, another form of wealth. When a customer deposits money in a bank, money in his hands, gets changed to deposit. In the books of the bank, a reverse change takes place. Wealth in the form of deposit gets changed to wealth in the form of money. Such changes of wealth are in trillions and cannot be listed in total.

When a buyer spends Rs.10 and buys a pen it is construed that the value of pen is Rs.10 or Rs.10 equals pen in value. One thinks that or at least one accounts that value of pen = value of money spent and wealth is neither created nor destroyed. When one observes change of wealth from one form to another, one notices that value of wealth of transferee form equals value of wealth of transferor form. This is, in principle, *Law Of Conservation Of Wealth.*

Mathematical Proof of Law of Conservation:

According to doctrine of mathematics, one can add like terms. One can add 2a and 3a and the answer is 5a. One can subtract 2a from 7a. The answer is 5a.

One cannot add 2a and 5b unless both are inter-convertible. One can add 3kg and 5kg. One can subtract 3kg from 5kg. One cannot add or subtract 2kg to/from 5 hours. If one assumes "a" as wealth and "b" as non-wealth, one cannot add/subtract non-wealth to/from wealth. This means that *Wealth Only Can Be Added To Or Subtracted From Wealth And Hence Wealth Can Neither Be Created Nor Be Destroyed But Can Be Changed From One Form To Another.* Further one can deduce that only wealth should be expressed in units of wealth.

Double Entry Book Keeping and Law of Conservation of Wealth:

When wealth changes from one form to another, value of transferor and value of transferee forms of wealth remain equal. Wealth can neither be created nor be destroyed but can be changed from one form to another. This Law of Conservation forms sum and substance of double entry bookkeeping. For any financial transaction, two entries are made simultaneously. One account is debited or in other words its balance is brought down and the other account is credited or in other words its balance is increased. The amount so debited equals amount so credited. That is value or amount of debit equals value or amount of credit. In a balance sheet one finds liabilities and assets. Liabilities are items or forms of wealth in units of money that the business owes and assets are the items or forms of wealth in units of money that the business entity is to receive. Liabilities are sources of money and assets are the application of money. In a balance sheet, true to Law of Conservation, one finds that liabilities = assets. Similar thing is noticed in other financial statements like receipt and payment, income and expenditure etc. At the end of the day when daybook or cashbook is closed it is seen that sum of debits = sum of credits. Thus according to Double Entry Bookkeeping method of accounting, wealth can neither be created nor be destroyed but can be changed from one form to another. This is ample proof for Law of Conservation of Wealth. This Law of Conservation proves further that items like goodwill, depreciation, loss that may not have Value in Exchange but are expressed in units of wealth and that are added to or subtracted from other forms of wealth are all forms of wealth. All the items that are shown in financial statements are forms of wealth.

Law of Conservation of wealth and definition of wealth:

Law of Conservation of Wealth helps define wealth. It is general notion that wealth is one that is scarce, wealth is one that has Value in Use and Value in Exchange. Items like Carbon dioxide, sunlight, chlorophyll, soil moisture, essential plant nutrients present in the soil may not have Value in exchange. They all join or combine to form Food that has Value in Exchange. According to doctrine of mathematics and also according to Law of Conservation of Wealth all these are forms of wealth. Wealth may or may not have Value in Exchange. Wealth may not be scarce either.

Law of Conservation of Wealth and Economics

Law of Conservation is the heart and soul of economics. One cannot imagine any law or theory in economics proposed by classical economists that is not
based on Law of Conservation. Without Law of Conservation, like all other sciences, economics becomes brittle and their theories drop like house of cards. This law gives credibility and acceptability to principles of economics.

In the first page of any book in economics, one finds terms "Wants" and "Means". Wants are the goods and services one wants to possess or own. Every individual has wants. Every family as an economic entity has wants. Every business enterprise has wants. Nation, association, organization and the human race in total have wants. To meet these wants there are "Means". Means are the money and money related forms of wealth. One must remember that wants and means are the two broad classes of wealth. There will be continuous reaction between wants and means. Wants get changed into means and means get changed into wants. When wealth changes from wants to means, the value of wants = value of means.

What if wants are more and means are few, as is in most cases? There are four likely possibilities that the economic entity adopt to bring about parity between wants and means. Let us study them.

1.   The economic entity substitutes costlier wants by cheaper wants so that wants and means become equal. When resources or means are few people tend to buy cheaper goods.

2.   The economic entity may postpone some wants and may satisfy only those wants that are compelling in nature. Here present wants are changed to future wants.

3.   The economic entity may raise loans the repayment of which is done through future means. In simple words, the entity cashes future means to fulfill present wants. In case the economic entity is state or nation, it may resort to fiscal deficit to make good the gap. Fiscal deficit is again a form of loan that the nation has to repay from its future means.

4.   The entity may sell some property that has use in future say a building or may resort to premature cashing of a term deposit. Here again future means are converted into present means to satisfy present wants.

If the means were to be more than wants reversal of what has been stated above can be witnessed. The economic entity substitutes costlier wants for cheaper wants or present means will be changed to future means by way of lending or by way of depositing in a bank or future wants gets changed to present wants. This confirms that the economic entity sees that wants and means are made equal. This is Law of Conservation of Wealth.

The above discussion goes to show that wants and means can be further classified as A) Present wants B) Future wants C) Present Means and D) Future means.

Economists use the terms "demand" and "supply". Are they forms of wealth? Simple words demand and supply are not forms of wealth. But if one expresses them in units of wealth, they assume the forms of wealth. Economists say that mere desire to buy does not constitute demand. In words of chemists, this is active concentration. When prices rise, demand contracts and as prices fall, demand increases. When prices fall, supply decreases and as prices move up supply improves. If one draws supply and demand curves, at the point of interception of these curves which is otherwise called equilibrium point, one finds that:

Value of demand in units of commodity = value of supply in units of commodity and Value of demand in units of money = Value of supply in units of money. This is n line with Law of Conservation of wealth. If demand increases the producers increase the production to meet the demand and conversely if supply increases demand increases. In the words of J.G. Say, supply creates its own demand. Thus Law of Conservation comes into play and ensures that value of demand = value of supply. If one expresses demand in units of money and supply in units of commodity, according to Law of Conservation of Wealth:

Value of demand (in money) = Value of supply (in units of commodity).

$$\therefore \ \frac{\text{Value of demand (in units of money)}}{\text{Value of supply in units of commodity}} = 1$$

Now one knows that, units of money ÷ units of commodity = *Price*. At a given price, value of demand in money terms equals value of supply in commodity terms. *This Is Law Of Conservation Of Wealth.* Thus entire study of demand and supply analysis is based on Law of Conservation. This concept is retold when one studies Quantity Theory Of Money.

The concept of Income, expenditure and savings is another theory one finds in economics that is truly based on Law of Conservation of Wealth. At times when wealth in the form of income changes into expenditure and savings, the value of income equals sum of the values of expenditure and savings. This is written as: Income = Expenditure + Savings. Further it is also said that Income = Savings + Expenditure + Taxes.

When one reverts back to earlier discussion, savings are the future means. Present means or "income" in this case has been changed to future means or "savings". There is neither creation nor destruction of wealth noticed here.

One classic example of application of Law of Conservation of wealth in economics is Quantity Theory of Money. According to this theory, at any given point of time, value of goods and services offered, equals value (Quantity) of money. As we have discussed earlier, goods and services are WANTS and money or money related forms are MEANS, value of wants = value of means and in other words, value of goods + services = value (or quantity) of money. While discussing demand and supply, we have proved that any given price, value of commodity (or service) = value of money. If commodity increases, price falls and if money increases price rises. Unfortunately, this Quantity Theory has received serious criticisms. But in support of this great Theory, one must say that this theory is based on Law of Conservation and hence cannot go wrong. Economists have not fully capitalized the advantages of this theory. Nowhere does one see economists viewing goods and services as *Wants* and money and money related forms of wealth as MEANS. The concepts of demand and supply and Quantity Theory of Money are overlapping in content.

Law of Diminishing Marginal Utility is again a Theory based entirely on Law of Conservation. This theory also received serious criticisms from successive economists although the theory is foolproof. According to William Stanley Jevans, Carl Menger , and Leon Walras, who independently put forth the theory, Utility is the satisfaction one gets by consuming a commodity. Marginal Utility is the satisfaction one derives from consumption of last unit of commodity. When a man is hungry and if he is provided with an apple (let us assume that the man likes apples) his satisfaction level by consuming the apple shall be high. But when the man is offered apples in succession, the satisfaction he gets from consuming each additional apple will be decreasing. Marshall has assumed numbers to represent satisfaction level. The incremental satisfaction that one derives by consumption of each successive unit of commodity is termed as "Marginal Utility" by Marshall. Every successive addition to a commodity results in less than proportionate increase in the utility. This is Law of Diminishing Marginal Utility. Keeping aside the critics raised against this theory let us understand how this theory is based on Law of Conservation of Wealth.

The foremost question is "whether utility is a form of wealth or not?" When one assumes utility as satisfaction, a term related mainly to human behavior, utility cannot be measured and hence falls short of being classified as wealth. Can this be corrected so as to make utility eligible for consideration as wealth? Yes. If one treats utility as human need, this lacunae can be overcome. When we say that there is need for 5 apples to fulfill our hunger, our need is expressed in units of wealth (apple). Human need has units and is generally expressed in units of wealth. Human need may be for goods and services or Wants as described earlier or for money and money related forms otherwise called as Means. Human need may have units of commodity or may have units of money. In the further discussion, wherever utility is mentioned it should be construed as human need.

When a man has utility for 5 apples, his utility = 5 apples. When he is given only one apple, and when he is unaware of receiving more apple/s, according to Law of Conservation, 1 apple = 5 apples. Marginal utility of this first apple is = 5apples ÷ 1 apple = 5. Marginal utility is a ratio and hence has no units. Marginal utility is taken as and construed as average utility here. Now, after consuming first apple, his need is reduced to four apples. If he is given an apple for consumption, according to Law of Conservation, this one apple = 4 apples and the marginal utility of this apple is 4. If, instead of one apple he is provided with two apples simultaneously, the situation would be, 2 apples = 4 apples and marginal utility = 2. Thus with successive additions the marginal utility comes down. When the man gets his 5th apple, the marginal utility is unity. After consuming 5 apples, his need is fully satisfied. At this point, utility equals to number of apples and any further addition will not result in increase in marginal utility.

There is another face of the coin. Human need is for means or money also. If means are spent for acquiring wants, marginal utility of means increases. At any given point, utility for commodity or wants = utility for means or money. In the chapter *Utility Complex* I have dealt in detail the composition of utility.

Law of Conservation leads us to one important concept. When matter changes from one form to another form and if change is in physical form e.g. water changing into ice, such change is called physical change. If the composition of the matter undergoes change, such change is called chemical change or chemical reaction. What should one call change of wealth from one form to another? I have termed them as *Economic Reactions*. As Law of Conservation and Law of Equilibrium apply to both matter and wealth, one finds common laws for chemical and economic reactions. One such law is Law of Mass Action that is more fully described in chemistry. Economic reactions and Law of Mass Action are more fully discussed in subsequent chapters of the book. Law of Conservation of Wealth is the mother of Double Entry Bookkeeping. Law of Conservation divides wealth into two distinct forms: Wants and Means. Always value of wants equals value of means. Law of Conservation is the mother

of various Economic laws or theories or concepts like Quantity Theory of Money, Law of Diminishing Marginal Utility, Law of Diminishing Marginal Returns, Income and Consumption Theory etc. All concepts, theories and laws of wealth originate from Law of Conservation and rightly end with Law of Conservation. Law of Conservation helps us define Wealth. Wealth is one that can be measured in known units of wealth, that can be changed to other forms of wealth and that can neither be created nor be destroyed. Wealth has two components: Value in Exchange and Value in Use. We may create or destroy Value in Exchange component of the wealth. But one must remember that value of wealth will not be destroyed. Value of wealth = Quantity of wealth × Equivalent value (or Value in Exchange). If the quantity of one form of wealth increases, due to law of Conservation, its relative value in terms of other form/s of wealth, which we call "Value in Exchange" decreases. This is the reason why forms of wealth like water, salt and air have low or no Value in Exchange. When quantity of one form of wealth decreases or its exchange value in terms of other form of wealth

increases. Wealth may lose its value when it is converted into wealth in the form of money but its value remains same when it is converted into other forms of wealth. A paper, with written matter on it, may not have value in exchange in money terms but when the same is used to produce heat energy, a form of wealth, it has value in exchange. There can be no matter or energy with zero absolute value in exchange and hence all forms of matter and energy are forms of wealth.

It is general notion that when a form of wealth that has Value in use is converted into a form of wealth that has value in exchange it is called Creation of Wealth. When a form of wealth that has value in exchange is changed into a form of wealth that has value in use we call it as destruction of wealth. In agriculture, forms of wealth like carbon dioxide, sunlight, chlorophyll, essential plant nutrients and water combine to form food, a form of wealth that has Value in exchange. Similarly, in a manufacturing industry, land, labor, capital and entrepreneurship combine to form finished goods, a form of wealth that has value in exchange.

Let me answer some common questions. Is not wealth lost when a house is burnt? Is not wealth lost when a shirt is torn? Is loss a form of wealth? Think that a house is burnt. The burning of house leads to release of light and heat. As for nature, both are wealth. Wealth here changed from house to wealth in the form of light and heat. It is true that we cannot make use of this wealth. Now, consider the utility of the remaining houses in the locality or the other houses owned by the same owner if any. There will be rise in the utility or marginal utility of remaining houses. The loss of this house or destruction of the house resulted in increase in the value or utility of remaining houses. Similarly when a shirt is torn, as far as nature is concerned, the quantity of matter used for the shirt remains unchanged and hence no wealth is lost. There is decrease in the utility of the shirt and this results in increase in utility of remaining shirts. Here again, the total utility remains same. This can be explained by the following equation:

4 shirts × Marginal utility of 4 shirts = 3 shirts × Marginal Utility of three shirts. Marginal utility here means utility per shirt. Since there is no word in place for this, marginal utility is used. The total utility or total value of shirts before and after tearing off of a shirt remains same. Since the marginal utility of shirts increases the economic entity buys shirt because:

Marginal Utility of Shirt is > Marginal Utility of Money. Thus there will be no loss of wealth.

Is loss a form of wealth?

Yes. Loss is a result of wealth being subtracted from wealth. Mathematically, when one subtracts 5a from 2a the result is −3a. Similarly when wealth of of higher value is subtracted from wealth of lower value we get loss. Loss is negative wealth. When wealth of lower value is subtracted from wealth of higher value we get profit, which is positive and if wealth of higher value is subtracted from wealth of lower value we get loss. Profit is a positive wealth and loss is a negative wealth. Loss is always expressed in units of wealth, say, Rupee or dollar or houses or shirts or quantity of crop etc. THERE ARE NO SEPARATE UNITS OF MEASUREMENT FOR LOSS. When one says sugarcane crop worth Rs.200000.00 is lost due to floods, wealth is expressed here in units of money.

In the strict sense the value in exchange for loss is the experience one gains from the economic reaction. What is the value of wealth? When wealth changes from one form to another, value of one form of wealth is stated or expressed in units of the other form of wealth. Value of wealth always depends on the economic use or the economic reaction the wealth undergoes. It also speaks the comparative usefulness of two forms of wealth. Value of wealth is like concentration. Always two forms of wealth are required to express value of wealth. When one says that value of 5grams gold is Rs.4500.00, two forms of wealth, gold and money are involved here. Value of gold is expressed in money terms and value of money is expressed in gold terms. In this comparative analysis, if value of one form of wealth increases, the value of the other form of wealth decreases. If quantity of one form of wealth increases, its value per unit decreases. It should always be borne in mind that Quantity × Value per unit of wealth A = Value of Wealth A = Quantity × Value per unit of Wealth B = Value of Wealth B.

Let us understand the words Use of wealth. It must be remembered that value of wealth always depends up on the use of wealth. When one says that he has spent Rs.2000.00 for purchase of a book, the wealth in the form of money has been changed here to wealth in the form of book. When a very intelligent man accepts a job or a profession not commensurate with his knowledge and skills, or in simpler words, owing to his need he does jobs less paying than his natural skills, his value is the one he has accepted to be. Here wealth is not lost but is put to unfair use. Similarly when a costly source of fuel like sandalwood is used as fuel, value of sandalwood would be equivalent to the fuel efficiency it has. Here again wealth is not lost but is not put to proper use and hence is not exchanged for due price.

One important concept needs mention here. Classical economists state that the system is always at full employment. Their sayings or postulates are in tune with Law of Conservation and also on the lines discussed above regarding value of wealth.

I.   *The wage is equal to the marginal product of labor*

That is to say, the wage of an employed person is equal to the value which would be lost if employment were to be reduced by one unit (after deducting any other costs which this reduction of output would avoid); subject, however, to the qualification that the equality may be disturbed, in accordance with certain principles, if competition and markets are imperfect.

II. *The utility of the wage when a given volume of labor is employed is equal to the marginal disutility of that amount of employment.*

That is to say, the real wage of an employed person is that which is just sufficient (in the estimation of the employed persons themselves) to induce the volume of labor actually employed to be forthcoming; subject to the qualification that the equality for each individual unit of labor may be disturbed by combination between employable units analogous to the imperfections of competition which qualify the first postulate. Disutility must be here understood to cover every kind of reason, which might lead a man, or a body of men, to withhold their labor rather than accept a wage, which had to them a utility below a certain minimum.

(Courtesy:
http://etext.library.adelaide.au.k/keynes/john_maynard/k44ghtml#chapter1)

One can understand from above postulates that value of wealth in the form of labor equals marginal product of labor. Marginal Product of labor is in the real sense marginal utility of labor for the employer. This is also equal to the marginal utility of wages for the employee when viewed from employee angle. At equilibrium point, marginal utility of wages for the employee equals marginal utility of labor for the employer. This is what is contained in Law of Conservation of Wealth. This is what is told when I say that value of wealth depends on its use. This further leads to conclusion that as classical economists put it, the society is always at full employment level. Law of Conservation is the mother of all these theories/postulates of classical economists. In simple words,

Value of labor = Value of wages and Utility of labor = Utility of wages. Further, Quantity of labor × Marginal Utility of Labor = Quantity of Wages × Marginal Utility of Wages.

$$\frac{\text{Quantity of Wages}}{\text{Quantity of Labor}} = \frac{\text{Marginal Utility of Labor}}{\text{Marginal Utility of Wages}}$$

Wages per labor is the ratio of marginal utility of labor to marginal utility of wages. When labor is in short supply, marginal utility of labor increases (refer Law of Diminishing Marginal Utility) and the result is increase in wages per labor. When marginal productivity of labor is high marginal utility of labor will be high. Under such circumstances also increase in marginal productivity helps increase wages per labor. When Marginal utility of wages increases, wages per labor decreases. This happens when people have more wants. When wants are more, requirement of means to fulfill the wants increase. When means (or wages) are not adequate or easy to come by, marginal utility of wages increases and hence people or the employee accepts job that is paying less. It is generally true that when wants are more and means are few, people or the employees accept less paying jobs or in other words wages per labor will be less. It is also true that in industries or sectors where marginal productivity of labor is more, marginal utility of labor will be more and this leads to increase in wages per labor.

This applies to services sector as well. In places where doctors are short in number, marginal utility of services of doctors increases and this leads to more earnings per doctor.

NOTES ON THE CHAPTER

1. Law of Conservation is a common law for matter, energy and wealth. Law of Conservation of Wealth can be stated as "When wealth changes from one form to another, value of transferee form of wealth is equal to the value of transferor form of wealth and that wealth can neither be created, nor be destroyed but can be changed from one form to another."

2. Law of Conservation is the mother of Double Entry Bookkeeping method of accountancy. According to the doctrine of Double entry bookkeeping, for every debit there ought to be credit of like amount and that we cannot create a debit/credit without corresponding credit/debit entry and further that assets should match liabilities, income should match expenditure and sources of funds should match application of funds.

3. All principles of economics and all theories of economics originate and end with Law of Conservation of Wealth. Law of Conservation like in double entry bookkeeping where one vouches correctness of accounting only when debits equal credits and assets match liabilities, is the acid test to vouch for correctness of a theory or a postulate.

4. Law of Conservation and Law of Equilibrium are two faces of a single coin. They never operate in isolation.

5. Law of Conservation helps us define wealth. Wealth may or may not have value in exchange. Wealth may or may not be scarce.

6. According to Law of Conservation when wealth changes from one form to another, Value of wealth A = value of Wealth B and Quantity of Wealth A × equivalent of Wealth A = Quantity of Wealth B × Equivalent of Wealth B. When there is increase in quantity of one form of wealth, its relative value in terms of other form of wealth (equivalent) decreases.

7. Loss is also a form of wealth as this is added to or subtracted to other forms of wealth and that loss is also expressed in units of wealth.

8. Value of wealth depends up on use of wealth. Use of wealth is nothing but the reaction the wealth undergoes or in other words the form of wealth it gets changed into. The wealth has many uses and the value most often differs from one use to the other.

CHAPTER IV

LAW OF EQUILIBRIUM AND MOVEMENT OF WEALTH

God has created matter, energy, wealth and soul. He has used minimal Laws and imparted similar properties to all the four. Law of Conservation of Wealth and Law of Equilibrium define every property of matter, energy, wealth and soul. Law of Conservation is the mother of all laws. When matter/energy/wealth change from one form to another, value/quantity/mass of transferor form equals value/quantity/mass of transferee form and that matter/wealth/energy can neither be created nor be destroyed but can be changed from one form to another. To enforce this Law of Conservation, Law of Equilibrium is in place. Whenever there is inequality in the value/mass/quantity of transferor and transferee forms of matter, Law of Equilibrium operates and brings about parity so that Law of Conservation is restored. In this chapter a detailed discussion is presented as to how this Law of Equilibrium operates.

When wealth changes from one form to another, say from wants to means, value of wants = value of means. This state is called equilibrium state. What happens if wants increase? How does this equilibrium state restored? Law of Dynamic Equilibrium helps restore this state. Therefore Law of Conservation and Law of Equilibrium always operate jointly and not in isolation. Law of Conservation is the cause and Law of Equilibrium is the effect. It is easier to understand the law if one studies how this law operates in systems of matter and energy.

When two systems of matter of different concentrations or levels are connected to one another, matter moves from higher concentration to lower concentration till equilibrium is achieved (or in other words concentration or level of matter in both systems equalize to be in conformity with Law of Conservation). Can one imagine equilibrium if matter moves the other way i.e. from lower concentration to higher concentration or level? No. Can equilibrium be achieved if matter moves at random? No. Let us consider the following example.

One must have seen air moving out of a vehicle tube when the tube bursts. Atmosphere contains more air than the tube but the level or concentration (in this case density) is lower than that of the tube. The factor that determines movement of air here is density and not the quantity of air. One must have read reasons for occurrence of winds. Air moves from high- pressure areas to areas of lower pressure and thus winds are formed. Many such examples may be quoted in support of this principle that matter moves from higher concentration to lower concentration.

Similarly when two systems of energy with different levels are connected with one another, energy moves from higher level to lower level till equilibrium is reached. Let me cite an example. Let hot water contained in a

Bucket is mixed with cold water contained in a tank. Hot water has a higher Temperature, or level of heat than that of cold water. Cold water may contain more heat energy than the hot water. From where does the heat move, from cold water to hot water or from hot water to cold water? Heat moves from hot water to cold water even though cold water has more heat energy than the hot water. Quantity of heat energy does not determine the course of movement of heat energy but the temperature or level of heat determines the course.

In economics, the concept of equilibrium is widely used. Adam Smith opines that invisible hands bring out equilibrium. Equilibrium concept is used in income, consumption and savings analysis, in demand, supply and fixation of price and in many other concepts. Unfortunately, the most important thing, the process by which equilibrium is restored is untold. Wealth, like matter and energy, should also move from higher concentration to lower concentration if equilibrium is to be achieved. The quantity of wealth is not the criteria for movement of wealth. The question that comes to ones mind foremost is "What is concentration of wealth?" When one says that concentration of sugar solution is 5%, one means that 5 grams of sugar is dissolved in 100 gram of solution. There are two distinct forms of matter here. Sugar, the form of matter otherwise called solute, and water, the form of matter that is otherwise called solvent, together form solution. To express concentration, two forms of matter are required. Similarly, to express concentration of wealth we need to have two forms of wealth.

Let us consider price as an expression of concentration of wealth. The two forms of wealth here are a) Money and b) Commodity or service. In rate of return, again a form of expression of wealth, a) return and b) investment are the two forms of wealth involved. In utility of money, the two forms of wealth are a) money and b) utility. In utility of commodity, two forms of wealth are a) utility and b) commodity. In cost of production, the two forms of wealth are a) cost and b) production. In wages, two forms of wealth are a) wages and b) labor. In case of rent, the two forms of wealth are a) rent and b) house or building or land. In exchange rate of currencies, the two currencies are the two forms of wealth. It is with this background let us study the concentration of wealth in detail.

When one says price of sugar is Rs.18.00 per kilogram, the numerator is unit of money and the denominator is unit of commodity or sugar in this case. Assume that there are two adjacent markets and the prevailing prices of sugar in the markets are as under:

Rs.16.00	Rs.17.00
Kilogram of sugar	Kilogram of sugar
Market A	*Market B*

The concentration of money is more in Market B because Rs.17.00 is greater than Rs.16.00. Sugar is concentrated in Market A because one kilogram per Rs.16.00 is greater than one kilogram per Rs.17.00. In cheaper markets, commodity is more concentrated and in costlier markets, money is more concentrated. Always one must remember that *concentration of one form of wealth is reciprocal of the concentration of the other form of wealth.* When one form of wealth is concentrated the other form will be dilute.

In the above example wealth in the form of money moves from Market B to Market A, as the concentration of money is higher in Market B than that in Market A. This means that buyers prefer to buy sugar from Market A rather than from Market B. Sugar is more concentrated in Market A than in Market B. Therefore sugar moves from Market A to Market B. Economists state the same concept in a different way. Economists say that buyers move from costlier to cheaper markets and commodities move from cheaper to costlier markets. Human behavior, though stated to be unpredictable, supports this principle of movement of wealth from higher concentration to lower concentration.

Example 2:

Let us consider another example. There are two houses in a same locality being offered on rent with similar built up area and comfort features. The rents quoted by the owners of the houses are as below:

Rs.4200.00 rent	Rs.4800.00 rent
House	House
House A	*House B*

The concentration of rent is more in House B than in House A. Therefore rent moves from House B to House A. In simple words, the hirers want to hire House A rather than House B.

Assume that you are a Production Manager of an industry. The unit is producing two products, Product A and Product B. Both the products have equal sales. You are asked to prepare production budget for a financial year. The costs and returns of the two products are as under:

Rs.48.00 costs	Rs.52.00 costs
Rs.100 Returns	Rs.100 Returns
Product A	*Product B*

The costs are more concentrated in Product B than in Product A because Rs.52 is greater than Rs.48.00. Therefore costs move from Product B to Product

A. In other words, you, the Product Manager allocate more resources for production of Product A than for Product B. In some of the cases, wealth moves in one direction only, as in the above case. Only costs moved and return remained static. In the earlier example of house being hired out, only rent moved and house remained static. Such movement of wealth is similar to a biological process called "*Osmosis.*" Since there is no term in place to describe movement of wealth of this kind, I have termed this as "*Osmotic Movement of Wealth.*"

When a semi-permeable membrane (a membrane that allows only solvent particles to pass through) separates two solutions of different concentration, solvent (particles) moves from higher concentration to lower concentration till the concentration of solvent on both sides becomes equal. This phenomenon is extensively used in food preservation. In this case, as solute particles are not allowed to pass through the semi-permeable membrane and only solvent particles are allowed to pass through, only one form of matter i.e. solvent moves. This process is clearly explained by an experiment called "Potato Boat Experiment." In this experiment, potato boat acts as semi-permeable membrane. When two solutions of sugar of different concentrations, say, 2% and 5% are separated by a semi-permeable membrane, say, potato boat (potato cut into shape of a boat), water (solvent) moves from 2% solution to 5% solution. If sugar particles were to move they would have moved from 5% solution to 2% solution. The semi-permeable membrane that separates the two solutions does not allow sugar particles to pass through. Since concentration of water is more in 2% solution water moves from 2% solution to 5% solution.

Let us consider some more examples of osmotic movement of wealth. Two banks are placed in a same locality and offer interest on deposits at following rates.

Rs.7.00 interest	Rs.6.50 interest
Rs.100 investment	Rs.100 investment
Bank A	*Bank B*

This is a case of osmotic movement of wealth. Interest is static. Only wealth in the form of investment moves. Rs.100 investment for Rs.6.50 interest is more than Rs.100 investment for Rs.7.00 interest. Therefore investment (or depositor) moves from Bank B to Bank A.

Imagine that you are working in a company that offers salary of Rs.15000.00 p.m. You are offered a post elsewhere for a salary of Rs.18000.00 p.m. The terms of service are same as in your present company. Do you mind joining the new company?

One labor	One Labor
Rs.15000.00 Salary	Rs.18000.00 Salary
Present Company	*Proposed Company*

This is a case of osmotic movement of wealth. Wealth in the form of wages or salary is immobile. One company does not pass on wages to other company. Only wealth in the form of labor or employee moves from company to company.

If salary were to move, the same would have moved from proposed company to present company. Wealth in the form of labor is more concentrated in present company because 1 labor ÷ Rs.15000.00 wages is greater than 1 labor ÷ Rs.18000.00 wages. Therefore it will be natural prudence that the employee shifts over to the new company. We notice that people move from jobs offering lower wages to jobs offering higher wages.

Let us assume that you are a bank manager and you have a credit proposal on hand. You have worked out Internal Rate of Return of the project using discounted cash flow statement. The internal rate of return is the rate at which the costs and benefits are to be discounted so that present worth of costs = present worth of benefits. The Financial analysts use the term Internal Rate of Return and Economists use the term Marginal Efficiency of Capital for the same concept. The opportunity cost of capital is, say 12%. The opportunity cost is the cost of foregoing other form of investment opportunity or in other words what the investment would earn if invested in other opportunities. The Internal Rate Return is 15%. Do you vouch for the financial viability of the project? It is generally agreed principle that IRR should be more than the opportunity cost to treat the project as economically viable. According to Law of Equilibrium wealth should move from higher concentration to lower concentration OR investment should move from opportunity cost to the proposed project to treat the project as viable.

Rs.100.00 Investment	Rs.100 Investment
Rs.12.00 Return	Rs.15.00 Return
Opportunity Cost	*Project*

From the above one can clearly see that wealth in the form of investment is more concentrated in opportunity cost than in the project. Therefore investment moves from opportunity cost to the project and hence the project is financially viable. Remember here again that wealth in the form of returns does not move one opportunity to the other. This is again a case of osmotic movement of wealth. Therefore it can be proved from above that for any venture or project to be financially viable, wealth in the form of investment should move from opportunity cost to the venture or project under consideration.

Let us assume that there are two nations interested in bilateral trade. The concentration of wealth in the two countries is as under:

$$\frac{US\,\$\,10000\ Billion\ Capital}{US\,\$\,100000\ Billion\ Natural\ Resources} \qquad Country \qquad A$$

$$\frac{US\,\$\,1000\ Billion\ Capital}{US\,\$\,5000\ Billion\ Natural\ Resources} \qquad Country \qquad B$$

If one observes capital, it is concentrated in Country A. If one considers natural resources, the same is concentrated in Country B. The natural course of movement of wealth would be, provided again that such movement is mutually acceptable to the nations:

Wealth in the form of capital moves from Country A to Country B and Wealth in the form of natural resources moves from Country B to Country A.

From the above example it will be clear that a poor country also has something to offer to a rich country.

People say that time is precious. I have in this book included a chapter "Time a form of wealth." Let us study whether time moves from higher concentration to lower concentration. All movements of wealth involving time as one form are Osmotic in nature since time does not move from one opportunity to another. Think that two banks offer following interest on deposits for following term or period.

$$\frac{181\ Days}{5.50\ \%\ interest} \qquad \frac{91\ Days}{5.50\%\ interest}$$
$$\qquad Bank\ A \qquad\qquad Bank\ B$$

Time is more concentrated in Bank A than in Bank B (181 days > 91 days). Therefore people prefer to deposit in Bank B rather than in Bank A or in other words, investment moves from Bank A to Bank B. This example can be retold substituting rent for interest and the effect would be same.

In the earlier chapter we considered utility as a form of wealth when utility is conceived in the meaning of human need. Does utility move from higher concentration to lower concentration? The utility has two components: wants and means. Human being needs goods and services that are otherwise called wants and he also needs money and money related forms of wealth that are called means. Utility is not a single form of wealth. It is a compound wealth.

$$\frac{Utility}{Wants} \qquad\qquad \frac{Utility}{Means}$$

If Utility ÷ Wants +is more than utility ÷ means, a situation where wants are more important, or in the words of economists, marginal utility of wants is more than marginal utility of money, people tend to buy the commodity or satisfy the want even by spending higher means. Conversely if utility ÷ wants is less than utility ÷means, i.e. when marginal utility of money is more than marginal utility of want or commodity, people do not buy the commodity. In such a situation, lowering of price would tilt the balance. By doing so, marginal utility of wants will be more than marginal utility of money and wealth in the form of utility moves from money to commodity. People buy the commodity. At equilibrium price, utility ÷wants = utility ÷ means or in other words marginal utility of commodity = marginal utility of money.

When there are two wants in consideration with different concentration of utility, the above concept repeats. Let me cite an example.

5 Units of Wants	7 Units of Wants
Rs.100 (Utility in means)	Rs.100 (Utility in means)
Want A	*Want B*

Utility is more concentrated in Want A than in Want B. Therefore people tend to buy or satisfy Want B rather than Want A. In the above example even if one assumes any other unit for utility the result would be same.

When wealth moves from higher concentration to lower concentration, one notices that any one or all of the following benefits result.

1. Decrease in costs
2. Increase in returns
3. Increase in profits
4. Decrease in losses
5. Increase in savings
6. Decrease in expenditure.
7. Increase in satisfaction

When wants are more and means are less, the relative value of means in terms of wants increase. In the reaction between wants and means,

Wants ↔ Means

When wants increase, if quantity of means remain same, wealth moves from wants (higher level) to means (lower level) thus decreasing the exchange factor of wants into means.

(Quantity × Equivalent Value) of Wants = (Quantity × Equivalent Value) of Means

When Quantity of one form of wealth, say A increases, wealth moves from that form of wealth to the other form of wealth, say B, thus reducing equivalent value of Wealth A, or increasing the equivalent value of wealth B. When supply of commodity increases, wealth moves from commodity to money and its equivalent value (or price) decreases or equivalent value of money increases. If houses increase in number, the equivalent value of houses in terms of rent or rent per house decreases. When laborers increase, wealth moves from laborer to wages and result is that the equivalent value of labor decreases or wages per laborer decreases. When quantity of Indian Rupee increases, wealth from Indian rupee moves to other currencies and the result is that the equivalent value of Indian rupee in terms of other currencies (Exchange rate) decreases. When Demand increases in quantity (may be in commodity terms or may be in money terms) wealth moves from demand to supply and the result is that the equivalent value of demand decreases or equivalent value of supply increases. This movement of wealth is the essence of Quantity Theory of Money. When money increases, wealth moves from money to goods resulting in increased equivalent of goods or price. Similarly, when goods and services increase, wealth moves from goods and services to money thereby increasing the equivalent value of money or reducing the price. All these movements are invisible or latent.

There are no exceptions to these God-made Laws and principles. The movement of wealth from higher concentration to lower concentration is a God-made phenomenon and hence has no exceptions. Human behavior has no say in this movement of wealth.

Law of thermodynamics says that any reaction that proceeds from higher energy to lower energy level is spontaneous. Similarly any economic reaction that proceeds from higher level of wealth to lower level of wealth is spontaneous. This should be the guiding factor for businessmen to promote sales. It should always be remembered that if marginal utility of goods or commodity is higher than marginal utility of money, sale takes place. When Marginal utility is more concentration of goods will be less (remember Law of Diminishing Marginal Utility). Similarly when Marginal Utility of money is less money is more concentrated. People buy goods when marginal utility

of goods is more than marginal utility of money or when money is more concentrated than the goods in the market. The role of advertisement is to create awareness among the people about the usefulness of a commodity so that its marginal utility increases. When Marginal Utility of Investments is higher than marginal utility of liquidity people invest or deposit money. If Marginal Utility of future means or money is more than marginal utility of present means or money people save.

When one agrees in principle that wealth moves from higher concentration one construe it as sufficient proof for Law of Equilibrium to be in operation. When one agrees Law of Equilibrium it is natural that one agrees Law of Conservation also. Thus it should be construed as important property of wealth that *Wealth Always Moves Move From Higher Concentration To Lower Concentration.*

NOTES ON THE CHAPTER

Law of Conservation and Law of Equilibrium are two faces of a same coin. Whenever there is imparity or Law of Conservation is off balance the Law of Equilibrium comes into force. The movement of wealth from higher concentration to lower concentration ensures equilibrium. This process is similar to movement of matter and energy. Quantity of wealth/matter/energy is not the guiding factor for this movement but the level or concentration or density of wealth/matter/energy   determines   the   course   of   movement   of wealth/matter/energy.

To express the concentration of wealth two forms of wealth are required. Concentration of one form of wealth is always reciprocal of the concentration of the other form of wealth. In some cases only one form of wealth moves and the form is static and I have termed such movement of wealth as Osmotic Movement of wealth and this process is similar to a biological process called Osmosis. When wealth moves from higher concentration we notice that there would be 1) increase in savings or 2) increase in income or 3) decrease in expenditure, or 4) Increased profits or 5) Increase in satisfaction or 6) all the above.

In an economic reaction, if there is increase in quantity of one form of wealth, wealth moves latently from that form of wealth to the other form of wealth and thus the relative value of wealth whose quantity remained unchanged increases. If goods increase in quantity, wealth moves from goods to money and that relative value of money increases and prices drop.

CHAPTER V
LAW OF MASS ACTION

In a chemical reaction, matter changes from one or more form/s to one or more form/s. There is no term in place to describe change of wealth from one or more form/s to one or more form/s. I have termed them as Economic Reactions. Economic reaction is a reaction where wealth changes from one/more form/s to one/more form/s. The economic reactions obey Law of Conservation and Law of Equilibrium. There is a general law that can be termed as subsidiary of these two laws and that this Law applies to all economic reactions. Since matter and wealth obey Law of Conservation and Law of Equilibrium, this Law, a Law originally established by chemists for chemical reactions, applies to all economic reactions. The name of this Law is Law of Mass Action. This law may be renamed as Law of Wealth Action to suit Economic Reactions. This Law embeds all existing economic theories or laws and is general in nature. One wonders why this law was first invented by chemists and not by economists. The study of this law simplifies the study of wealth.

Law of Mass Action of chemical reactions

This law is about rate of chemical reactions. In any reversible chemical reaction, the rate of reaction is directly proportional to the product of the concentrations of reacting substances expressed in moles per liter (when one gram molecular weight of a substance is dissolved in one liter of water we call the concentration as one mole per liter for e.g. when 98 grams of sulfuric acid is dissolved in one liter of water we call the concentration of sulfuric acid as one mole per liter).

Let us assume that $A + B \leftrightarrow C + D$ is a reversible chemical reaction where A and B are reactants and C and D are products .The rate of forward reaction is proportional to concentration of reactants i.e. A and B. If concentration of A and B increases, the rate of forward reaction increases i.e. more units of A and B get converted into C and D. The rate of reverse chemical reaction depends on concentration of C and D. If concentration of C and D increases, rate of reverse reaction increases and more units of C and D get converted into A and B. Let [A] and [B] are concentrations of A and B respectively. Let [C] and [D] be concentrations of C and D respectively. The rate of forward reaction is proportional to [A] and [B]. Let K1 be the proportionality constant of this forward reaction. Then,

Rate of forward reaction = K_1 [A] [B]

Similarly let K2 be the proportionality constant of reverse reaction.

Rate of reverse reaction = K_2 [C] [D]

At equilibrium point, rate of forward reaction is equal to rate of reverse reaction.

K_1 [A] [B] = K_2 [C] [D]

One can deduce further that:

$$\frac{K_1}{K_2} = \frac{[C][D]}{[A][B]}$$ K_1/K_2 is a constant and we can call it K.

$$K = \frac{[C][D]}{[A][B]}$$

Thus, if concentration of A and B increases, K decreases but K being constant, it will be restored by more units of A and B getting converted into C and D thereby concentration of C and D increases.

This Law of Mass Action is of great importance in reactions involving change of wealth. This Law encompasses all economic activities and provides foolproof answer to several hitherto unknown issues facing economists. This Law is GENERAL and applies to all forms of wealth. It would be appropriate to call this Law as Law of Wealth Action. All existing economic theories like Quantity Theory of Money, Law of Diminishing Marginal Utility and Law of Diminishing Marginal Returns are just the limited versions of this general law. One cannot imagine any economic theory that is not a subsidiary of this general law. Since this Law has its feet firmly grounded on Law of Conservation, this law is flawless.

When one form of wealth, say "A," changes into another form of wealth, say "B," the reaction can be written as:

A ↔ B

The rate of forward reaction is proportional to the quantity of Wealth A.

Let K_1 be the proportionality constant of forward reaction.

Rate of forward reaction = K_1 × Quantity of Wealth A.

Similarly, rate of reverse reaction is proportional to quantity of Wealth B.

Let K_2 be the proportionality constant of reverse reaction.

Rate of reverse reaction = K_2 × Quantity of Wealth B.

At equilibrium point rate of forward reaction equals rate of reverse reaction. At equilibrium, $K_1 \times$ Quantity of Wealth A = $K_2 \times$ Quantity of Wealth B AND

$$\frac{K_1}{K_2} = \frac{\text{Quantity of Wealth B}}{\text{Quantity of Wealth A}}$$

As in chemistry, K_1 / K_2 are a constant and may be denoted as K. This K is the equilibrium constant for economic reactions. If quantity or concentration of A increases more units of A get changed into B or in other words rate of forward reaction increases. If concentration of B increases, more units of B get changed into A or in other words rate of reverse reaction increases. The equilibrium constant, K, here is given by:

$$K = \frac{\text{Quantity (or concentration) of Wealth B}}{\text{Quantity (or concentration) of Wealth A}}$$

The equilibrium constant K has no particular meaning in chemistry. In Economics this K assumes different meanings in different reactions.

Example 1: In the reaction of sale/purchase (when one sells the other buys and hence sale and purchase should be treated as single reaction), wealth in the form of commodity gets changed to wealth in the form of money and conversely, in the hands of the buyer, wealth in the form of money gets changed to wealth in the form of commodity. The reaction here is:

Commodity ↔ money

$$K \text{ the equilibrium constant, } = \frac{\text{Quantity of Money}}{\text{Quantity of Commodity}} = Price$$

We know that quantity of money/quantity of commodity is price. As quantity of commodity undergoing reaction increases, rate of forward reaction increases and more units of commodity get changed into money resulting in fall of price. If quantity of money undergoing this economic reaction increases, rate of reverse reaction increases and more units of money get changed into commodity and the result is increase in price.

The above concept is told in different ways in economics. Quantity Theory of Money states that value of goods and services offered equals money supply and that increase in money supply leads to increase in price. If demand is expressed in units of money and supply is expressed in units of commodity, it is generally accepted principle that as demand increases price increases and as supply increases price falls. Chemists and economists agree that only active concentration or quantity should be considered. Economists say that mere desire to buy does not constitute demand. Similarly chemists say that the actual active concentration of reactant/product is important. Chemists treat water as universal solvent and the concentration in chemistry means quantity of a substance dissolved in one liter of water. In economics, utility or human need is the universal solvent in which almost every form of wealth dissolves. Thinking that there is equal need for money and commodity, one can ignore the utility (or the denominator) and substitute quantity for concentration.

Example 2: Let us consider another reaction,

$$Investment \leftrightarrow Liquidity.$$

Investments are of various types. Investment may be in the form of depositing money in a bank, investment may be in the form of purchasing government securities, may be in the form of treasury bills, may be in the form of investing in shares and debentures, may be in the form of capital, etc. Let us consider first investment in the form of bank deposits.

Liquidity $\leftrightarrow$ *Bank deposit*

Liquidity here means the face value of the deposit and bank deposit here means maturity value of the investment.

$$K = \frac{Maturity\ Value}{Face\ Value}$$

Maturity value ÷ face value is *compounding factor* (if compound interest is paid on deposits).

$$Compounding\ factor = [1 + (\frac{r}{100})]^n$$

Here n is number of quarters or years if compounded quarterly or yearly as the case may be. "r" is the rate of interest.

If liquidity increases or if face value of deposit increases compounding factor decreases. When a system has sufficient liquidity, deposits are rather easy to come by and this results in decrease in compounding factor. Compounding factor is a function of rate of interest and as compounding factor decreases, rate of interest decreases. When liquidity is scarce, rate of interest increases and when liquidity is abundant more units of liquidity get changed to deposits and hence compounding factor, K, decreases and the effect is reduction in rate of interest. Many financial analysts have vouched the same at various times. This concept applies to investment in government securities and treasury bills as well. If liquidity increases, in the reaction,

$$Liquidity \leftrightarrow Government\ security,$$

the increased quantity or units of liquidity results in increased rate of forward reaction or in other words increased quantity of liquidity gets changed into government security. This results in increase in price of government security thus reducing yield on government security or K. This concept is explained in detail with this reaction:

Liquidity (or purchase price of security) ↔ Security (or unit of security sold)

$$K= \frac{\text{Security or Investment (Face value)}}{\text{Liquidity or amount spent on purchase of security}}$$

If liquidity were abundant, by spending more liquid assets one would get security of lesser face value. In other words, prices of securities move up when liquidity is abundant and when liquidity drains out from the system the prices of securities fall. This concept applies to stock markets as well. When liquidity is abundant prices of shares are on the rise. Decline in liquidity brings out decline in share prices.

If K drops (due to excess liquidity in the system) the equilibrium will be restored by movement of wealth and equilibrium gets restored. Between the two broad classes of wealth; wants and means, means are more active and are more mobile. Generally liquid wealth or means move from higher concentration to lower concentration till the equilibrium is reached.

Example 3: Let us consider another important reaction. In Economics there is a very important Law called The Quantity Theory of Money. According to this law, value of goods and services offered equal money supply. The basic equation of Quantity Theory is:

MV=PQ

Where M is the stock of money, V the average number of times the money is used, P the price index and Q the goods exchanged for money. This V is of no significance in the study of wealth because all economic reactions are reversible in nature and whenever money changes, goods and services also change. If one assumes goods and services as Wants and money supply as Means this theory encircles entire Economics. Unfortunately it is not viewed so.

This theory, as one can see, is purely based on Law of Conservation. The left hand side equals right hand side. The value of transferor form of wealth, say money, equals value of transferee form of wealth, say goods and services. Hence, whatever counter arguments are by some economists against this noble theory, this theory is foolproof.

In the reaction, money ↔ goods + services,

As money supply increases, according to Law of Mass Action, the rate of forward reaction increases. More units of money get changed to goods and services and hence price rises. If goods and services increase in quantity, rate of reverse reaction increases and more units of goods and services change into money. Thus prices drop.

$$K= \frac{\text{Quantity of Money}}{\text{Quantity of goods and services}} = \text{Price}$$

If quantity of money increases, rate of forward reaction increases and thus more units of money get changed to goods and services resulting in increased price. If goods and services increase, more units of goods and services change into wealth in the form of money (or rate of reverse reaction increases) resulting in decrease in price. As price decreases, demand increases and price is restored. If prices increase, supply or quantity of goods and services increase and equilibrium is restored.

Example 4: Let us consider the reaction involving change of wealth from one currency to another.

US $ ------------------ $\rightarrow$ Indian Re

$$K= \frac{\text{Quantity of Indian Rupee}}{\text{Quantity of U.S.\$}} = \text{Exchange Rate}$$

If quantity of US Dollar increases, more units of US $ get converted into Indian Rupees or rate of forward reaction increases and the K, the equilibrium constant decreases. If on the other hand, Indian Rupee increases, the rate of reverse reaction increases and Indian rupee loses its exchange value. One reads occurrence of this phenomenon in newspapers daily due to change in the quantity of one or both the currencies.

Example 5: Houses are rented out. The tenants pay rent for using the house. House and rent are forms of wealth. In the reaction,

House ---------- $\rightarrow$ Rent

$$K= \frac{\text{Quantity of Rent}}{\text{Quantity Or Number of Houses}} = \text{Rent Per House}$$

If houses available for hiring out in an area increase, the result would be the rent per house or K or equilibrium constant decreases. If the tenants in an area afford to pay more rent, the rate of reverse reaction increases and more units of money or rent get changed into house thus increasing the rent per house or K. There is a concept of Quasi Rent in Economics. When houses are less in number, the rent per house will be higher than normal or equilibrium Level. This increase in rent is called Quasi Rent. When rents are high people prefer to invest in housing sector thus increasing the number of houses in a locality and equilibrium is brought out.

Example 6: Costs are incurred in a production firm or in a business firm to earn returns. The costs are said to be of three types: a) Non-recurring or Fixed Costs, b) Recurring or Variable costs and c) semi-variable costs. There are some costs that are partly fixed and partly variable and these are termed semi-variable costs. Let us consider the reaction involving costs and returns.

Costs ------------------ $\rightarrow$ Returns

$$K = \frac{\text{Quantity of Returns}}{\text{Quantity of Costs}}$$

It is prudent thinking that returns should be more than costs. The state at which costs and returns are equal is termed as BREAK EVEN POINT. At this point K, the equilibrium constant shall be equal. Initially when costs are more and returns are less K is small. As returns increase rate of reverse reaction increases and returns are pooled back into the firm's business as costs. The return: cost ratio is unique for every industry or business. Generally equilibrium is reached soon. Generally, in industries or business involving greater risk or skill or both the return: cost ratio will be high.

Example 7: If one substitutes cost by capital, a factor of production, one arrives at an important Law of Economics called Law of Diminishing Marginal Returns. Increase in capital or any factor of production results in decrease in the marginal returns or returns from the additional capital or factor of production. Assuming all other factors remain same, an increase in one factor of production results in less than proportionate increase in returns. Let us observe this phenomenon using Law of Mass Action.

Capital ------------ → *Returns*

$$K = \frac{\text{Returns}}{\text{Capital}} = Marginal\ Return\ of\ Capital$$

As Capital increases, more units of capital get changed to returns, or rate of forward reaction increases resulting in reduction of marginal returns. After some time, returns increase and rate of reverse reaction increases and equilibrium is restored. This K, the equilibrium constant is generally industry specific.

Example 8: Labor is an important form of wealth employed in production or business. Wages are the forms of wealth the laborer gets for having lent his labor. In this reaction,

Labor ------------- → *Wages*

$$K = \frac{\text{Wages}}{\text{Labor}}$$

If number of laborers increase, number of laborers rendering their services increase, or rate of forward reaction increases and wages per laborer or K, the equilibrium constant, decreases. If the firm or the system is in a position to pay higher wages, rate of reverse reaction increases and the result is increase in wages per laborer. This is the reason why the wages are more in developed countries. This is also the reason for higher wages noticed in Indian villages during seasonal agricultural operations. Now that outsourcing has become order of the day and the gap is narrowing down. Labor is the least mobile of the factors of production. If mobility improves one sees that equilibrium will be reached much sooner.

Example 9: We often come across this reaction:

Income --------→ Expenditure

$$K = \frac{\text{Expenditure}}{\text{Income}}$$

Income gets changed to expenditure and one man's expenditure is other's income. As Income increases, spending increases or more units of income get changed to expenditure and the result is decline in K, the equilibrium constant or Marginal Propensity to consume as is called in economics. Due to conversion of income in to expenditure, quantity of expenditure increases and the rate of reverse reaction increase. This again is a short- lived phenomenon and equilibrium is reached by various ways. The economic entity may raise the standard of living and may buy costlier products. The economic entity may resort to savings and thus quantity of income undergoing this reaction comes down.

Example 10: In this reaction,

Income ←→ Tax

$$K = \frac{\text{Tax}}{\text{Income}}$$

We notice that as Income increases, the rate of forward reaction increases and the ratio of Tax to Income decreases. This is the reason perhaps behind advocacy of progressive taxation. Again, as tax increases, more tax gets converted into income and equilibrium is restored. The tax one pays is the income for the state. As Income increases, the rate of effective taxation, K, or Tax : GDP ratio decreases. In developed countries where GDP is high, rates of taxes are low.

Law of Diminishing Marginal Utility and Law of Mass Action:

In economics, there is classic theory called Law of Diminishing Marginal Utility. This Law is highly criticized for the assumptions it makes. However there is general agreement that this Law is a guiding factor for various economic activities. There are attempts to free the utility concept from behavioral or psychological hold. Utility is the satisfaction one gets from consuming a commodity or good. One cannot measure this utility.

Law of Diminishing Marginal Utility states that every increase in consumption of a commodity results in less than proportionate increase in Utility or successive consumption of a commodity results in decreased satisfaction. There are some questions here: 1) Is utility, a mental phenomenon, measurable? 2) Is utility a form of wealth? Are there any modifications or changes in the concepts that impart these properties to wealth? Yes. Assume that utility is all that a human being needs or requires. Now this utility acquires the properties of wealth. Let us study in detail.

Think that a man is hungry and needs five apples to satisfy his hunger. His utility is expressed here or measured here in units of apple, a form of wealth, and it is equal to five apples. When the man consumes apples, his utility is changed to apples and apples are changed to utility (remember double entry bookkeeping). Thus, utility, in the meaning of human need, acquires properties of wealth and becomes a form of wealth. When utility becomes a form of wealth the Law of Diminishing Marginal Returns can be tested for its correctness and applicability.

In the discussions that follow utility is used with the meaning of human need. The marginal utility is considered to mean utility per unit of wealth (be it commodity, be it money or be it a service). It is not confined to utility of the last consumed commodity or last spent money as economists put it. It is wrong to call it average utility either. I hope that economists pardon me for using the word in this sense. There is no word in place for *Utility Per Unit Of Wealth* and hence the word Marginal Utility is used to mean this measure. This applies to marginal product of labor, marginal returns etc., wherever the word marginal is used. In economics, word marginal relates to consumption or production of last unit of commodity.

Think that a man is hungry and needs five apples to satisfy his hunger. His utility is 5 apples or this can be written as: 1 utility = 5 apples. Think that he is given one apple and that he is unaware of any further supply of apples. The reaction here is:

1 apple $\leftrightarrow$ 1 utility (5apples)

$$K = \frac{5 \text{ apples } (1 \text{ utility})}{1 \text{ apple}} = \text{Marginal utility of first apple} = 5$$

When first apple is served and that the man is not aware of any further apples coming his way, he equates the first apple with the total need or utility. According to Law of Conservation, Value of transferor form of wealth equals value of transferee form of wealth and in this case, 1 apple = 1 utility or 5 apples. If he were told that he would receive some more apples, this would certainly not be the case. Thus the marginal utility of first apple is five according to Law of Mass Action.

Now after consuming one apple the need for apples or hunger comes down to four apples. Think that he is provided with another apple. The reaction would be:

1 apple $\leftrightarrow$ 4 apples or 1 utility

$$K = \frac{4 \text{ apples} \, (1 \text{ utility})}{1 \text{ apple}} = \text{Marginal utility of first apple} = 4$$

For the third apple, marginal utility becomes three and similarly the fourth apple shall have marginal utility of two. As man consumes more and more apples, the marginal utility goes on increasing. Due to successive consumptions, the need or requirement of apples comes down and the result is decrease in marginal utility for every successive addition of apple.

Assume that the man was given two apples at a time. This would have resulted in the following reaction:

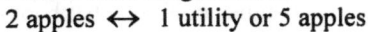

2 apples $\leftrightarrow$ 1 utility or 5 apples

According to Law of Mass Action,

$$K = \frac{1 \text{ Utility Or 5 Apples}}{2 \text{ apples}} = 2.$$

After consuming two apples the utility will be reduced to three apples. If he were served with two more apples,

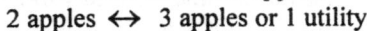

2 apples $\leftrightarrow$ 3 apples or 1 utility

$$K = \frac{3 \text{ apples Or 1 Utility}}{2 \text{ apples}} = 1.5$$

For the next two apples served simultaneously, the average marginal utility becomes 1.5.

A reverse process happens in case of marginal utility of money. Successive spending on apples reduces cash on hand and naturally marginal utility of money increases. Price is the ratio of marginal utility of commodity to marginal utility of money.

From all the above examples some conclusions can be drawn. As quantity of one form of wealth increases its relative value in terms of the other form of wealth decreases. The equilibrium constant, K, is the relative value of one form wealth in terms of the other form of wealth. Observe the following:

A) As quantity of goods or services increase, price, the relative value of goods and services in money terms decreases. If quantity of money increases, its relative value in goods terms decreases or prices rise.

B) If number houses increase its relative value in terms rent decreases. If rent offered is increased rent per house increases.

C) If quantity of costs increases, relative value of costs in returns terms decreases.

D) If liquidity increases its relative value in terms of investment decreases.

E) If number of laborers increase, wages per laborer decreases.

When one plots wealth in the form of reactant along x-axis and wealth in the form of product along y-axis, equilibrium constant, K, is the slope of the line we get.

$$K= \frac{\text{Quantity of Product}}{\text{Quantity of Reactant}}$$

By cross multiplication,

K X Quantity of reactant = Quantity of product.

Left hand side i.e. K X Quantity of reactant is the value of wealth in terms of the product.

Quantity of Product X 1/K = Quantity of Reactant.

1/K or multiplicative inverse or reciprocal of K is the value of product in terms of the reactant. An increase in value of one form of wealth results in reduction in its relative value in terms other form of wealth. At any point, Quantity × Value of wealth A = Quantity × Value of Wealth B. This is in simple words LAW OF CONSERVATION OF WEALTH. This is the reason why substances or forms of wealth like water, air, salt etc that are abundantly available have low value in exchange.

Now what if more than one form of wealth undergoes reaction to form more than one form of wealth? Think that there are three types of liquidity in the market: short term liquidity, medium term liquidity and long- term liquidity. Let us denote them as L1, L2 and L3. Assume that there are types of investments, say short term, medium term and long term investments. Let us denote them as I1, I2 and I3.

In the reaction,

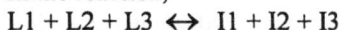

L1 + L2 + L3 ↔ I1 + I2 + I3

According to Law of Mass Action, The rate of reaction is proportional to the product of concentration of reacting substances. In chemistry, water is the accepted universal solvent. Majority of the substances dissolve in water. Is there any such form of wealth that dissolves almost all other forms of wealth? Yes. The Utility or human need or human requirement is the form of wealth in which all other forms of wealth dissolve. Utility, the human requirement can be expressed in units of money, in units of commodity or in any other unit of wealth. Suppose a man needs Rs.1000.00 the utility here is Rs.1000.00 and it is expressed in units of money here. In the Law of Mass Action what shall be the ideal unit of utility? In chemistry the unit of measurement of water is liter or 1000 c.c. Let us make a beginning assuming Rs.1000.00 as unit of utility. Let us study some of the examples we have already dealt with.

$$\frac{5 \text{ Kg. Potato}}{\text{Rs.1000 utility}} \quad \text{Reacts with} \quad \frac{\text{Rs.25.00 Money}}{\text{Rs.1000 utility}}$$

$$K= \frac{\text{Rs.25 Money per Rs.1000 Utility}}{5 \text{ Kg. Potato per Rs.1000 utility}} = \text{Rs.5 per Kg. Potato}$$

From the above, we notice that the utility being common to products and reactants utility gets nullified. Let us analyze further:

The numerator Rs.25 money / Rs.1000 utility is the Reciprocal or Multiplicative inverse of Marginal Utility of Money (Marginal Utility of Money = Utility / Money). The denominator, 5 Kilogram Potato / Utility is Reciprocal of Marginal Utility of Potato. Therefore, K, the equilibrium constant is the ratio of Marginal Utility of Commodity (potato in this example) to Marginal Utility of Money. If, in the reaction goods -→ money, concentration of goods per 1000 utility increases (or in other words Marginal utility or utility per unit of good decreases) there will be fall in price. If concentration of money per 1000 utility increases (or in other words marginal utility of money or utility per unit of money decreases) there will be rise in price.

Let us apply the concept of concentration of wealth in utility to other reactions. In the following example: $\dfrac{\text{Labor}}{1000 \text{ Utility}} \rightarrow \dfrac{\text{Wages}}{1000 \text{ Utility}}$

$$K = \frac{\text{Wages Per 1000 Utility}}{\text{Labor per 1000 Utility}}$$

$$K = \frac{\text{Marginal Utility of Labor}}{\text{Marginal Utility of Wages}}$$

Conclusion: If marginal utility of labor increases, wages per labor or K increases. If Marginal Utility of Wages increases there will be decrease in wages per labor. Wages per labor is the ratio of Marginal Utility of Labor to Marginal Utility of Wages.

In the reaction, Houses ↔ Rent, Rent per House is the ratio of Marginal Utility of Houses to Marginal Utility of Rent. If Marginal Utility of Houses increases rent per house increases and if Marginal Utility of Rent increases, rent per house decreases.

In the reaction, Income ↔ Expenditure, K, the equilibrium constant, or Marginal propensity to consume is the ratio of Marginal Utility of Income to Marginal Utility of Expenditure. When Income is less marginal utility of income is more. If Marginal Utility of Income increases, there will be increase in Marginal Propensity to Consume. If Marginal Utility of Expenditure increases, there will be decrease in Marginal Propensity to Consume.

When wants are more, one observes that marginal utility of income will be more. In such cases income will be converted in to expenditure more rapidly and Marginal Propensity to Consume or K or Expenditure/Income will be high. According to Keynes Multiplier, Income = Multiplier × Public expenditure.

When Government spends Re1 this amount spent becomes income for the other. Consider that the recipient of this money saves Re.0.10 and spends Re.0.90. The Marginal propensity to consume in this example is 0.90. The amount so spent forms income for a third person. Assume that he spends Re.0.81 (0.9 × 0.9) and saves Re.0.09. This Re.0.81 so spent becomes income for a fourth person. Thus in the chain down below, the amount of Re.1 spent by the Govt. result in cumulative income of Rs.10 (Re.0.9 + 0.81 + 0.72 + 0.64 + 0. 58 + 0.52 + 0.47 + -----). When Marginal Utility of Income is more, People attach more importance to Income and therefore Expenditure gets changed to Income. When Marginal Propensity to Consume is high every unit of money spent by the Government as public expenditure results in an increase in cumulative income.

In the reaction, Costs ↔ Returns, K, the equilibrium constant, or returns per unit of cost, is the ratio of Marginal Utility of Costs to Marginal Utility of Returns. When Marginal Utility of Costs is high or when costs are dearer Returns per unit of cost will be high. Marginal Utility of Costs will be high when Opportunity Costs are high. This applies to Capital --→ Returns as well. If Marginal Utility of capital is high, Returns per capital will be high.

In the figure illustrated here, one can observe that if level of reactants increase, wealth moves from reactants to products or rate of forward reaction increases. If level of products increase, rate of reverse reaction increases. If quantity of one form of wealth increases, its rate of convertibility in other form of wealth decreases.

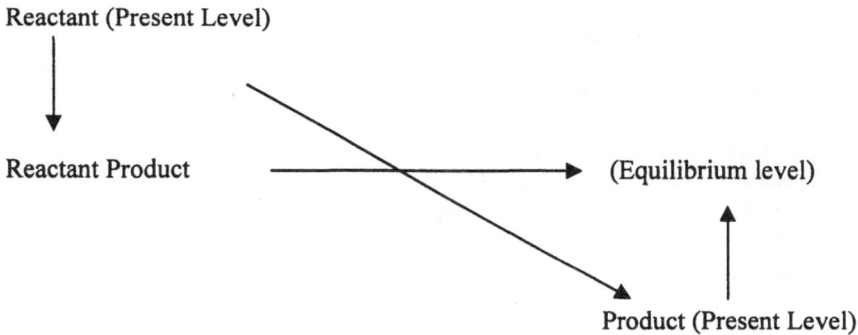

Fig.1: When concentration of wealth in the form of reactant or in other words quantity of reactant form of wealth is more than concentration or quantity of product form of wealth, wealth moves latently from reactant to product till such time that the concentration or value of wealth on both sides becomes equal.

Increase in quantity of reactant wealth results in movement of wealth from reactant to product or higher concentration to lower concentration. Assume that market is equilibrium at 500 quintals of potato and Rs.40000.00 money. Think that there is addition in supply of the commodity. Potato is wealth and hence cannot be destroyed. This increase in wealth or potato results in increase in value of money. Wealth moves from potato to money and correspondingly value of money increases. But since potato becomes cheaper here buyers from neighboring markets come and buy potato thus restoring equilibrium.

Let us revert to the situation where more than one form of wealth reacts to form more than one form of wealth, i.e.

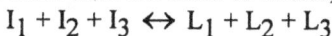

$$I_1 + I_2 + I_3 \leftrightarrow L_1 + L_2 + L_3$$

Let us consider the concentrations of the reactants and products.

$$\frac{L_1}{1000\,Utility} + \frac{L_2}{1000\,Utility} + \frac{L_3}{1000\,Utility} = \frac{L_1 + L_2 + L_3}{1000\,Utility}$$

Taking LCM,

$I_1 + I_2 + I_3$ = Short Term Investment + Medium Term Investment + Long Term Investment = Total Investment

$L_1 + L_2 + L_3$ = Short Term Liquidity + Medium Term Liquidity + Long Term Liquidity = Total Liquidity

Thus the equilibrium constant, $K = \dfrac{Total\ Investment/1000\ Utility}{Total\ Liquidity/1000\ Utility}$

Thus, in a reaction involving change of wealth from two or more form to more than one form, the rate of reaction is directly proportional to the sum of the quantities of reacting substances. The equilibrium constant is the ratio of Marginal Utility of Total Reactants to Marginal Utility of Total Products. When there is increase in Marginal Utility of Liquidity, equilibrium constant K increases. This results in increase in the yield of the investment. When Marginal Utility of Investment increases, there will be decrease in equilibrium constant K. This results in decrease in yield of the Investment.

Let us consider one more example:

Tomato + Potato + Beans ↔ Money

You have gone to vegetable market to buy vegetables. Think that your need for vegetables, expressed in units of money, is Rs.100.00. You end up buying the three vegetables or the equilibrium constant K here is:

$$K = \frac{[Tomato + Potato + Beans\,]/100\ U}{Money\,/100\ U}$$

According to Law of Diminishing Marginal Utility and Hicks indifference curve analysis, man wants to maximize his satisfaction under available conditions or resources. This is possible only when Marginal Utility of quantities of potato, tomato and beans equal marginal utility of money. As Hicks said there might be many possibilities for this which he calls points of indifference.

Advantages of Law of Mass Action (Law of Wealth Action):

1.   This Law is general and applies to all forms of wealth and all changes involving forms of wealth.

2.   This Law is foolproof. This Law has its roots firmly anchored in Law of Conservation and Law of Equilibrium. This Law is free from faults.

3.   This Law is easy to understand and this law simplifies study of economic reactions.

NOTES ON THE CHAPTER

In short one can summarize that, in any economic reaction, the rate of reaction is directly proportional to the quantity of reacting form of wealth.

When quantity of reactant form of wealth increases, there will be increase in the rate of forward reaction. More units of wealth in the form of reactant change into wealth in the form of products. Conversely, when the quantity of product form of wealth increases, rate of reverse reaction increases and more units of products change into reactant form of wealth.

If quantity of one form of wealth increases, without corresponding increase in the quantity of other form of wealth, its relative value in terms of the other form of wealth decreases. This law is comprehensive and is applicable to all reactions involving change of wealth from one form to another.

CHAPTER VI
ECONOMIC REACTIONS

When matter changes from one form to another, such change is called physical change or chemical change depending on the nature of change. If the composition of the matter is not altered, such a change is called physical change. Example: Water changing into steam. If composition of the matter undergoes change such a change is called chemical change example: burning of wood. Here wood combines with oxygen and carbon dioxide and ash are formed. Chemical change is also called as chemical reaction.

In one's daily life, one comes across several instances of wealth changing from one form to another. All financial transactions involve change of wealth from one form to another. Sale is the commonest example of change of wealth from one form to another. No special term is in place to describe such change of wealth from one form to another. Hence the term, "Economic Reaction" is proposed by me to express such change of wealth from one form to another. In my book titled Economic Reactions I had introduced the concept and the Journal of Economic Literature in their September 2004 edition accepted the concept of Economic Reactions.

Chemical reactions are of two types. Some are reversible and some are irreversible. When A and B react to form C and D, A and B are called *Reactants* and C and D are called *Products*. In some reactions, say, burning of wood, A and B react to form C and D but C and D do not react to form A and B. When wood is burnt an irreversible reaction takes place. Wood and oxygen combine to give carbon dioxide, ash and water. But carbon dioxide, ash and water do not give us wood and oxygen back. Such reactions are called Irreversible Reactions. In such cases, reaction proceeds in only one direction. In some reactions, A and B react to form C and D and C and D in turn react to form A and B. Such reactions are called REVERSIBLE reactions. The unique characteristic of economic reactions is that *All Economic Reactions Are Reversible In Nature*. This is the base for *Double Entry method of Bookkeeping*. There ought to be a credit of like amount for every debit and converse is also true.

When a buyer buys a product, we observe that in his hands, wealth in the form of money changes into wealth in the form of product. In the hands of the seller, wealth in the form of product changes into wealth in the form of money. Thus wealth in the form of reactant changes into wealth in the form of product and conversely, wealth in the product changes into wealth in the form of reactant.

How to write Economic Reactions? Since this concept is new, one can follow the system of chemists in writing chemical reactions. There are two symbols used by chemists: A) "→" and B) "=." The sign = is used to denote that the two forms of matter are equal in mass (in tune with Law of Conservation of Mass). The sign → is used to denote irreversible reactions. A reversible reaction is generally expressed using sign "↔." The same denotation can be used to express economic reactions.

Let us practice writing some economic reactions. This concept is not new to accountants and bankers since they write many such reactions.

1. When a commodity is bought or sold, wealth in the form of money gets changed to wealth in the form of commodity in the hands of the buyer. In hands of the seller, wealth in the form of commodity gets changed to wealth in the form of money. This reaction can be written as: money ↔ goods or goods ↔ money. Generally, the form of wealth written on the left side of equation is called Reactant and that written on the right side is called Product.

2. When a person deposits money in a bank, in his hands, money is changed to wealth in the form of deposit. In the hands of the banker, wealth in the form of deposit is changed to wealth in the form of money. This can be written as: money or cash ↔ deposit.

3. When income is changed to expenditure + savings, the reaction can be written as: Income ↔ Expenditure + Savings.

4. When one puts in his labor and earns wages or salary, the reaction can be written as: Labor ↔ Salary or wages.

5. When a house is hired out, the economic reaction can be written as: House ↔ Rent.

6. When one currency, say Rupee, is changed to another currency, say US Dollar, the reaction can be written as: Re ↔ US $.

Chemical Reactions and Economic Reactions

1. In chemical reactions, matter changes from one form (or more forms) to one or more other form/s. In economic reactions wealth changes from one or more form/s to one or more form/s.

2. Majority of the chemical reactions are irreversible in nature. All economic reactions are reversible in nature. This is the reason why there ought to be a credit of like amount for every debit in Double Entry Bookkeeping method of accounting.

3. In a chemical reaction, substances react with each other in the ratio of their equivalent weight. Say, when calcium reacts with oxygen, 20grams of calcium (equivalent weight of calcium expressed in grams) reacts with 8grams of oxygen (equivalent weight of oxygen is eight). In an economic reaction, one form of wealth reacts or replaces another form of wealth in the ratio of utility equivalent or price equivalent or cost equivalent or return equivalent (you may add some more to the list). When wealth in the form of goods is changed to wealth in the form of money the reaction takes place in the ratio of price equivalent. If the price of potato is Rs.5.00 per Kilogram of potato, money amount Rs.5.00 reacts or replaces one kilogram of potato.

4. Law of Mass Action is an important Law applicable to chemical reactions. This Law is applicable to *All Economic Reactions* as well. In economics there are many theories related to individual economic reactions. To cite a few, one may mention Quantity Theory of Money, Law of Diminishing Marginal Returns etc. All these are limited versions of Law of Mass Action. There is no single Law in Economics that is general to all forms of wealth and that describes in total the rate of economic reactions. One may rename this Law as Law of Wealth Action to suit economic reactions.

5. In chemical reactions, the medium or the solution is such that reactants have limited options or in other words, the place where chemical reaction takes place is small and only a few reactants take part in the reaction. In economic reactions, reactants have vast options. The medium may be enlarged vastly to cover entire globe. In economic reactions the reactant may be in India and the product may be in USA. Money may be made to react simultaneously with various types of goods, services and investments. This makes the study of wealth interesting. Due to movement of wealth, wherever there is gradation in concentration of wealth, wealth either rushes in or goes out. Unfortunately people account this for social aspect and behavioral aspect of wealth. Because economic reactions are many times more in number than chemical reactions, accurate analysis is difficult.

6. Chemists use some techniques to speed up chemical reactions. They are, in principle, applicable to economic reactions as well.

7 Using chemical reactions, a person is enabled to find out the unknown concentration or quantity of a reactant. The formulae $N_1V_1 = N_2V_2$ is useful to find out the unknown concentration or quantity of reactant or product. This formula is extremely helpful to know the concentration or quantity of reacting wealth as well. Some examples of the use of the formula are covered later in the chapter.

Thus chemical reactions give insight into the nature, properties and laws of matter. Similarly economic reactions help us understand the nature and properties of wealth.

Economic reactions help one determine value of wealth. Value of wealth largely depends on the use it is put into. The use of wealth is nothing but the economic reaction it enters into. When one says that one has bought a commodity by spending money, it means that wealth in the form of money is changed into wealth in the form of commodity and that the money is put into use for buying the commodity. Similarly, when a man hires out his house, we notice that wealth in the form of house changes into wealth in the form of rent. When a machine is used to produce a commodity, wealth in the form of machine changes into wealth in the form of produce and it is otherwise the depreciation. A form of wealth may be put to different uses and such use determines the value of wealth. Sandalwood has many uses. It can be used for woodcarvings, for religious ceremonies, for making furniture, for fuel etc. If it is used for artistic works or in a religious ceremony; its value will be high. The same sandalwood if used as a fuel, has less value. Its value will be measured in terms of its fuel efficiency. Similarly, an intelligent man may work for smaller salary. Value of his labor depends on the job he performs. It is the *Use* or the ECONOMIC REACTION the wealth enters into determines the value of wealth.

Based on this we can classify economic reactions into four categories.

1.   In the first kind of reaction, wealth that has Value in Use is converted into wealth that has Value in Exchange. The examples for this kind of economic reactions are: Photosynthesis, industrial production and the work of an artist (here his skill, a form of wealth that has Value in use is converted into a piece of art that has value in exchange.) In such cases, one is made to believe that wealth is created but in reality wealth only changes forms.

2.   In the second reaction, wealth in the form of Value in exchange is changed to wealth in the form of value in use. All types of consumption and expenditure are of this type. Food, a form of wealth that has value in exchange, on consumption, changes into energy, a form of wealth that has value in use to our body.

3.   In some reactions, say financial transactions like depositing money in a bank wealth in the form of value in exchange changes into similar kind of wealth, i.e. into one that has value in exchange.

4.   In some reactions, wealth changes from one that has value in use to wealth that is of similar kind, i.e. value in use.

CONCEPT OF EQUIVALENT

In chemistry, one finds an important concept called Equivalent weight. When two substances react, they react in the ratio of equivalent weight. To illustrate with an example: 40 grams of sodium hydroxide reacts with 49 grams of sulfuric acid or 36.5 grams of hydrochloric acid. The equivalent weight of sodium hydroxide is 40 and that of sulfuric acid is 49.

The equivalent weight of hydrochloric acid is 36.5. Similarly, when oxygen reacts with calcium it will be in the ratio of 8 grams of oxygen and 20grams of calcium. The equivalent weight of oxygen is 8 and that of calcium is 20.

When economic reactions are considered one finds that this concept is applicable to economic reactions too. But, there are many names for this concept.

Price equivalent, exchange equivalent, return equivalent, cost equivalent, utility equivalent etc. are the names one can give to this concept of equivalent weight of chemistry. Let us study in detail.

In a reaction of sale/purchase, goods get exchanged or react with money in the ratio of price. If the price of a commodity is Rs.6.00 per kilogram, one kilogram of commodity replaces or reacts with or gets exchanged for Rs.6.00. Price is the measure of equivalence. Currencies of two countries get exchanged in the ratio of exchange equivalent. If the rate of exchange of US $ is Rs.43.26, one US $ gets exchanged for Rs.43.26 Indian Currency. What is Utility equivalent? If utility of a commodity is 1 utility = 6 kilograms and if the utility of money is 1 utility = Rs.120.00, commodity and money get exchanged in the ratio of 6 kilograms: Rs.120.00. Utility is a measure of human need. It is rightly said in economics that price is the ratio of marginal utility of money and marginal utility of commodity. This simply means that marginal utility acts as equivalent weight. Return equivalent is an important factor that determines price of Government securities, treasury bills etc. If in a market, yield on securities is 5.37% pa and if the coupon rate of a Government security is 6.05%, the price of the security gets adjusted such that the yield on security will be 5.37%.

The equivalent concept leads us one formula of chemistry. This formula is $N_1V_1 = N_2V_2$. N_1 and N_2 are the concentrations of reactants expressed in Normal concentration. When one gram- equivalent of a substance is dissolved in one liter of solution, we call the solution as one Normal solution. To illustrate with an example, if 40 grams of sodium hydroxide (equivalent weight of sodium hydroxide is 40) is dissolved in one liter solution we get sodium hydroxide solution of one Normality. In chemistry, it is proved that one gram equivalent of a substance always reacts with one gram equivalent of another substance. V_1 and V_2 are the volumes of the reactants.

In an experiment, a solution of sodium hydroxide of 0.1N concentration of 10ml reacts with 10.2ml of hydrochloric acid of unknown concentration. We want to know the concentration of hydrochloric acid. This can be found out using the formula $N_1V_1 = N_2V_2$. N_1 is the concentration of sodium hydroxide and this is known to us to be 0.1N. V_1 is the volume of sodium hydroxide and is known to be 10ml. V_2 is the volume of hydrochloric acid that is determine by experiment to be 10.2ml. N2 is the concentration of hydrochloric acid that we are required to know.

$$N_2 = \frac{N_1V_1}{V_2} = 10.0 \times 0.1 \div 10.2 = 0.098 \text{ N}.$$

In economic reactions also one form of wealth reacts or replaces other form/s of wealth in the ratio of equivalence. This can be used to solve many problems of economic reactions. Let us solve some problems.

Think that the exchange rate of US $ in rupee is Rs.43.25. You know the rupee equivalent or Exchange rate of pound sterling in Indian rupee and let that be one pound sterling= Rs.76.00. You are interested in knowing exchange equivalent of US $ in pound sterling. Here exchange equivalent of US $ = N_1 = Rs.43.25 and exchange rate of pound sterling = N2 = Rs.76.00. V_1 is volume or quantity of US $ and this is unity. We want to know V_2, i.e. volume or quantity of pound sterling we would get from one $.

$$N_1V_1 = N_2V_2$$
$$43.25 \times 1 = 76.00 \times V_2$$
$$V_2 = 43.25 \div 76.00 = 0.5691 \text{ Pound sterling}$$

Example 2: An Investment say "A" gives 5% returns. Another investment "B" gives 4% returns. A man has invested Rs.30000/- in Investment A. To earn same returns what should be the quantum of investment in Investment B?

N_1 = Rate of return in Investment A = 5% OR 0.05
N_2 = Rate of return in Investment B = 4% OR 0.04
V_1 = Volume of Investment A = Rs.30000.00
V_2 = Volume of Investment B =?

$$V_2 = \frac{N_1V_1}{N_2}$$

$$= 30000 \times 0.05 \div 0.04 = Rs.37500.00$$

Example 3: A firm produces two products. The return per unit of product A is Rs.39.00. The return per unit of product B is Rs.42.00. The company produces 2000 units of Product A. This year the company wants to substitute product B for product A. To earn the same returns how many units of Product B be produced by the firm?

N_1 = Return equivalent of Product A = Rs.39
N_2 = Return equivalent of Product B = Rs.42
V_1 = Volume of Product A produced = 2000 units
V_2 = Volume of Product B to be produced =?

$$V_2 = \frac{N_1V_1}{N_2} = \frac{78000}{42} = 1857.1$$

One can use this formula for various other examples. The basis for operation of this formula lies in Law of Conservation of wealth.

N_1V_1 = Equivalent × Volume or quantity of Wealth A = Value of Wealth A.

Similarly, N_2V_2 = Equivalent × Volume or quantity of Wealth B = Value of Wealth B.

According to Law of Conservation of Wealth, when wealth changes from one form to another, value of transferor form of wealth equals value of transferee form of wealth. Therefore, Value of wealth A equals value of wealth B and $N_1V_1 = N_2V_2$

This formula leads us to one important conclusion. Let N1 be marginal utility of goods. Let N_2 be the marginal utility of money. Let V1 be the quantity of goods. Let V_2 be the quantity of money. $N_1V_1 = N_2V_2$

From this one can deduce:

$$\frac{N_1}{N_2} = \frac{V_2}{V_1}$$

$$\frac{\text{Marginal Utility of Commodity}}{\text{Marginal Utility of Money}} = \frac{\text{Quantity of Money}}{\text{Quantity of Commodity}} = \text{Price.}$$

Price is the ratio of marginal utility of commodity and marginal utility of money. If the marginal utility of commodity is higher than that of money prices rise. If marginal utility of money is higher than that of commodity, prices fall. Marginal utility is the ration of quantity of commodity required to the quantity of commodity present. If one needs 10 apples and if only two apples are available the marginal utility here would be 5.

Speeding up Economic Reactions:

Can one speed up economic reactions? Every businessman and every marketing personnel must be really interested in speeding up the economic reaction called SALE. In this reaction, goods and services get changed to money. Are there any techniques to speed up the reaction? Yes. There are some techniques used by chemists to speed up chemical reactions. These apply to economic reactions as well.

I)By reducing the particle size by powdering or by grinding:

Chemists finely grind the particles of reactants so that particle size of reactants comes down. Grinding or powdering of particles helps increase surface area. By reducing particle size one is increasing surface area of the particles. This concept is difficult to digest for social scientists and needs elucidation. Take one kilogram of wheat and grind it into flour. Observe the space occupied by the two. One notices that wheat floor occupies more space than the wheat. If one observes the space occupied by sand and clay it is evident that clay, a soil particle with finer size, occupies more space than sand, a coarser soil particle. Let us examine the concept mathematically.

Take a cube of side 1meter and break into cubes of side ¼ meter. We observe that we get 64 cubes of side ¼ meter from one cube of side 1meter. Calculate the surface area of the bigger and smaller cubes.

The surface area of the cube with side 1 meter = 6 × 1 × 1 square meters = 6 sq. meters. The surface area of 64 cubes of side ¼ meter = 64 × 6 × ¼ × ¼ = 64 square meters. Thus by reducing particle size from side 1 meter to ¼ meter, surface area increased from 6 square meters to 24 square meters or four fold increase was noticed. Increase in surface area facilitates better contact of reacting particles and the reaction speeds up.

What is surface area for an economic reaction, say sale? MARKET is the surface area for an economic reaction. It is here that reacting constituents or sellers and buyers interact. By reduction in particle size or unit quantity of commodity sold, does the market expand? YES. One must have noticed that retail sellers and buyers are many times more in number than the wholesale buyers and sellers. If one wants to sell a large piece of land perhaps buyers may not easily come by. If the land is split into smaller pieces, there will be many buyers. This concept is properly made use of by FMCG (Fast Moving Consumer Goods) industry. We notice that shampoo, hair oil, toothpaste etc are now sold in sachets. This has benefited the FMCG industry.

II) By stirring, mixing or shaking chemical reactions are speeded up

By stirring or by shaking the particles of reactants come in close contact and the reactions speed up. Similarly to speed up economic reactions, the reactants should be properly mixed. In other words, the reactants must be brought nearer so that reaction would take place faster. The news media is an important source where people, buyers and sellers, know each other. They also come to know the prevailing prices, the shortfall or adequacy of supply of a commodity, its current demand, the alternative uses the commodity can be put to use etc. Brokers and middlemen also do the job of mixers and shakers. Many a times, a deal will not be possible without their intervention. The material must be lifted from places where there is no demand to places where there is greater demand

III) By preparing solutions of reactants chemical reactions are speeded up.

Materials in dry states generally do not react with each other. Chemists prepare solutions of the reactants so that the reactants readily react with each other. Matter or solute in a solution is homogenously spread and has the requisite mobility. Similarly, it is good to prepare solution of wealth to speed up economic reactions. One needs a good solvent for this. The solvent is UTILITY. Unless a substance or a form of wealth dissolves in utility or human need it will not react with other forms of wealth. There is a second line of thought here. In a solution, particles of reactants are homogenously spread and are highly mobile. By ensuring proper transportation economic reaction may be speeded up. In these days of Internet, it is easier to transfer wealth in liquid form. Money and money related forms are liquid forms of wealth and hence are quick to react compared to goods and services.

IV) By use of catalysts chemical reactions can be speeded-up.

Chemists use substances called catalysts to speed up chemical reactions. There are substances called enzymes that are biological catalysts speeding up biochemical reactions. These catalysts do not take part in chemical reactions but create situations conducive for chemical reactions.

Advertisements are the important economic catalysts that speed up economic reactions. They do not take part in economic reaction. Some chemical reactions do not proceed in the absence of a catalyst. Similarly it is impossible to think of marketing a product in the present scenario without advertisement.

V) By increasing the temperature or pressure or both chemical reactions can be speeded up.

Heating the reactants improve the speed of chemical reactions. Increasing pressure may also be necessary to speed up chemical reactions. When reactants are heated, There will be increase in the energy level of reactants. According to Law of Thermodynamics any reaction that proceeds from higher energy level to lower energy level is said to be spontaneous. By increasing the temperature or pressure the energy level of reactants increases and this facilitates progress of the reaction. When there are famines, floods or other natural calamities the consumer fears shortage of goods and services. Even during days of war or political uncertainty people fear shortage of goods. A pressure will be created in the minds of the public and people try to hoard or stock the commodity for future use. This enhances speed of the economic reaction. Here again, when future price of a commodity is expected to be more than the present price, the present concentration of goods will be more than the future concentration of goods. So, as wealth moves from higher concentration to lower concentration wealth in the form of present goods changes to wealth in the form of future goods thus speeding up the economic reaction.

PROPERTIES OF ECONOMIC REACTIONS

The important properties of economic reactions are: In an economic reaction wealth changes from one or more form/s to one or more form/s. All economic reactions are reversible in nature. This is the reason we have Double entry bookkeeping method of accounting. When wealth changes from reactant to product, it is certain that a reverse reaction involving change of wealth from product to reactant takes place simultaneously.

In any economic reaction, the value of reacting forms of wealth equals value of product form of wealth. This is in simple words Law of Conservation of Wealth. This is the reason why the debits should match credits in bookkeeping and further that assets should match liabilities. This leads us further to the conclusion that wealth can neither be created nor be destroyed but can be changed from one form to the other. If there is imbalance or inequality in quantity or exchange value or both of reactant and products the same will be brought to equal by Law of Equilibrium.

Law of Equilibrium ensures that the values on both sides are equal. Movement of wealth from higher concentration to lower concentration ensures equilibrium. Value of wealth = Quantity of wealth x Equivalent of Wealth. This equivalent of wealth is the conversion factor of one form of wealth to the other or this is the value of one form of wealth in terms of the other form of wealth.

In any economic reaction, $N1V1 = N2V2$ where $N1$ is equivalent of wealth A and $V1$ is the quantity or wealth A. $N2$ is the equivalent of wealth B and $V2$ is the volume or quantity of wealth B. Generally, price and marginal utility are the measures of equivalence. By decreasing unit size of the reacting forms of wealth one can speed up economic reactions. .Any reaction that proceeds from higher level of wealth to lower level of wealth is spontaneous. A man buys a commodity if the marginal utility of the commodity is high. When commodity is less concentrated its marginal utility of commodity will be high (remember Law of Diminishing Marginal Utility). Similarly when marginal utility of money is low, money is more concentrated. In such case wealth (at buyer's end) changes from money to commodity i.e. from higher concentration-money to lower concentration- commodity.

NOTES:-

In one's daily life one comes across several instances where wealth changes from one form to another. Such reactions are termed as economic reactions. Buying and selling, depositing money in bank, all accounting transactions etc are examples of economic transactions. All economic reactions are reversible i.e. reactants are changed to products and conversely products are changed to reactants. When a commodity is bought, wealth in the form of money is changed to wealth in the form of commodity in the hands of the buyer and a reverse reaction takes place simultaneously in the hands of the seller. This is the reason why we have a debit for every credit in double entry or in other words this property of wealth has ensured success of Double Entry Method of Bookkeeping. The economic reactions have some similarities with chemical reactions.

The concept of equivalent applies to economic reactions as well. In other words forms of wealth react in the ratio of their marginal utility or price or returns or costs as the case may be. Wealth is neither created nor is it destroyed in a reaction. The value of wealth on both sides of the reaction remains same. Economic reactions can be speeded up. Making smaller the unit size of the reactants, advertisement, proper mobility of reactants, reducing price or increasing marginal utility or both, prevalence of external threat etc. helps speed up economic reactions. It is prerequisite that wealth should be soluble in utility to undergo economic reaction.

CHAPTER VII

UTILITY COMPLEX

Utility, as defined earlier, means all that a human being needs. A man has needs. A family has needs. A society has needs. A firm has needs. An organization has needs. A state or a nation has needs. The needs of human beings can be classified into wants and means. These wants and means are centered in the brain/decision making body of a man organization or family or state or company or any economic entity one may think of. The wants are large in number. To meet these wants there are means. Wants and means together constitute needs. The system is complex in nature. Hence I have termed this center where needs and means are placed or dealt with as Utility Complex. This center is like a cell of a living organism or an atom of an element. In this fundamental or basic unit that wants and means react. Many cells join to form a tissue and many such tissues join to form a body. Similarly, utility complex of individuals in a family join to form utility complex of the family. Utility complexes of individuals in a society combine to form Utility Complex of the society.

To understand this complex phenomenon it would be better if one understands structure of water. Water and utility complex have some basic similarities.

1)   Water is a form of matter and utility is a form of wealth. Utility is the human need or human requirement. This utility can be expressed in units of other forms of wealth. When a man needs 5meter cloth his utility is expressed as 5 meters cloth.

2)   Water has chemical composition of H_2O. Two atoms of hydrogen combine with one atom of oxygen to form one molecule of water. In aqueous state water is in the form of H^+ and OH^- (one hydrogen ion with a positive charge and one hydroxyl ion with a negative charge). Similarly, Utility also has two components. It is not made up of one form of wealth. There are two distinct components of this utility. Wants and Means are the two components of utility. Every economic entity has wants comprising of goods and services and to fulfill these wants economic entity needs means (money or money related forms of wealth). God has created all things, living or otherwise, abstract or concrete, using two

opposite charges or characters. Male and female, positive and negative, wants and means, are the examples. The God has seen that these forms are equal and opposite. He has also ensured that like characters or like charges repel each other and the opposite characters attract each other. Positive charged particle repels another positively charged particle. In magnets, south- pole of one magnet repels south- pole of another magnet. One want repels other want. One item of means repel other means. Wants and means attract each other. Distilled water, a form regarded as pure, contains equal concentration of H^+ and OH^- ions. Such a solution is called neutral solution. If in a Utility Complex, where wants and means are. equal in concentration, one may call the Utility Complex as one in Saturated State. If hydrogen ion concentration increases in a solution, we call the solution as acidic. If hydroxyl ion concentration increases we call the solution basic or alkaline. Similarly, if wants are more than means one may call the utility complex as poor and if the means are more than wants one may call the utility complex as rich.

In an atom, protons, those with positive charge do not move. Electrons, those with negative charge move. In a utility complex, wants are immobile. Means move from one utility complex (one atom) to another (atom). Hence it would be appropriate to assume negative charge to means. Means are always expressed in units of money. Examples of means are: cash, bank deposits, shares, debentures etc. Accountants have rightly called these as liquid assets considering their mobility.

(3)   Water is considered as universal solvent. Many substances dissolve in water. This character of water has made water a very important substance for all living beings. For smooth progress of any biochemical reaction, the reactants should be in solution form. When one thinks of utility, utility is form of wealth in which almost all forms of wealth dissolve. This makes utility the most important form of wealth for human life. The speed of any chemical reaction is rapid if the reactants are in the form of a solution. For any economic reaction to progress, it is prerequisite that the reactant forms of wealth must be soluble in utility. When a company launches a new product, it should ensure that the product is soluble in utility or human need. In other words, only those products that have utility are sold or bought.

(4)   Water exhibits cohesive and adhesive properties. One water molecule attracts other water molecule and one of the results is capillary force. Water molecule attracts molecules of other substances. Water is used as adhesive. This is largely due to the composition of water. As water exists in H+ and OH- form, water has acquired adhesive and cohesive properties. Similarly, utility exhibits adhesive and cohesive properties. Utility attracts other utility and utility attracts other forms of wealth.

(-) Means Wants (+)		(-) Means Wants (+)
Utility Complex A		*Utility Complex B*

Wants of one utility complex, a substance with a positive charge, attracts means of another utility complex, a substance with a negative charge. Think that Utility Complex A is of a buyer and Utility Complex B is of a seller. Buyer depends on seller for goods or to fulfill his wants and where as seller depends on buyer for his means. Thus two utility complexes (means of seller and wants of buyer in this case) are attracted or bound to each other. When a buyer wants to buy, he has need for the substance (or wants) he is buying. Simultaneously the seller is selling the substance. He has need for money or means. The wants of one utility complex bind the means of another utility complex. The charges of utility complexes bind utility complexes.

Solubility of a form of wealth in utility is influenced by various factors. One important concept that is common to chemistry and economics is *Common Ion Effect*. When two substances of different solubility and with some common ions are present in a solution, the solubility of the less soluble substance decreases resulting in precipitation of the substance. In a solution, say two salts, Na Cl (sodium chloride) and $CaCl_2$ (Calcium chloride) are dissolved. Sodium chloride ionizes into sodium ion with a positive charge

and chloride ion with a negative charge. Similarly calcium chloride ionizes into calcium and chloride ions. The chloride ion is a common ion for both the salts. In such situations, the solubility of less soluble salt, calcium chloride in this case, decreases. This is called common ion effect. This concept is very important from business management perspective. When there are more cars in middle- income segment, the car with greater utility eliminates other cars. All these cars cater to the needs of same class of consumers. They have common thing that they are priced similarly. The car with more utility, that is, the car with better style, better technology or better mileage makes other cars in the market insoluble in utility. They precipitate and they may sometimes are thrown out of the market.

Similarly, there is one more concept called diverse ion effect in chemistry. If there are goods catering to different segments of the society or satisfying different needs of consumers, one enhances the solubility of the other in utility. People buying a car or a motorcycle also buy television and washing machine. Car and washing machine satisfy different needs of the consumer.

A substance, say car, may satisfy more than one want. Car satisfies wants like a mode of transport, a symbol of class, a picture of taste etc. There are few substances that satisfy only one want. The poor sees many utilities in the things he buys or consumes, where as for the rich, the things they buy satisfy fewer wants or needs. When wants are more and means are few, man buys such goods or services that satisfy more than one want. When means are more he buys such goods or services, say a precious piece of art, that satisfy one or fewer wants. Unfortunately this concept is also similar to a principle in chemistry called Dilution effect and concentration effect. In a dilute solution, divalent and trivalent ions are preferentially adsorbed to mono valiant ions. If the concentration of means is dilute, as in the case of poor and the middle class, divalent or trivalent ions, the commodities that satisfy more than one wants are preferred to commodities that satisfy single want. When the concentration of means increases, as in the case of the rich, the commodities that satisfy a single want, say a piece of art, is preferentially adsorbed to commodities that satisfy more wants. It is the greatness of the God that he has used same principles for chemistry, a material science, and for economics, a subject considered to be behavioral and social in nature.

Is equilibrium good? We know that at any point of time, according to Law of Conservation, the wants and means equal each other. When wants are more than means, we notice that any or all of the following take place..

(a) Cheaper wants replace costlier wants:

(b) Present wants get changed to future wants, in other words the economic entity postpones buying the goods or service:

(c) Future means are changed to present means (by availing loans or by cashing long term assets or by resorting credit purchases which are to be repaid from future means).

(d) What if means were abundant and wants are few? One sees reversal of the processes stated above. One notices that a) costlier wants substitute cheaper wants: b) present means are changed to future means by making long term investments in banks or in stock markets or in real estates etc.:

(e) Future wants are changed to present wants i.e. the economic entity starts storing things or commodities that are needed in future.

I remember a story that I read in a Kannada Monthly. With due apologies to the writer I submit that I do not know the name of the author and volume of the magazine. A youth is sleeping, on a hot sunny afternoon under a tree in a public garden. A man of middle age passing by the youth makes notice of this and having annoyed of laziness of the youth, starts preaching the youth the importance of hard work. The youth asks innocently, as to what he would get if he works hard. The middle- aged man says "you would get money. The money would get you worldly comforts. You can buy food, shelter, clothing and all that you desire." "Then?" asks the Youth. "You can work at your will and rest at your will. You will be your OWN boss." says the Middle-aged man. The youth replies" What am I doing now? I am working at my will and resting at my will. For this small thing why should I work hard?" The story ends here. But think for a while that the youth acts on the advice of the middle aged man. He would never attain his goal in life. This state of genuine laziness would certainly have eluded him.

Think that a clerk in a Government office aspires for promotion in his career. It is generally an accepted notion that as one climbs up the ladder he would be paid more. An in depth study would reveal that as one moves up the ladder it is in deed true that he will have basic comforts and money, but it will also be true that he will have to work more. Think that the clerk is promoted to officer cadre. He has to work hard. Think that he is promoted further up and he becomes a Manager. He has to work harder. Think that he becomes General Manager or Chief Executive Officer. He will have no time to rest. There will be few to question him if he rests but he can't. He will have money. He will have comforts. He will have personal attendants but hardly has any time to think of it. As one moves up in the cadre, he will be more active. The richest man may perhaps be the busiest man in the world. As one moves up, he will have money, he will have comforts and he will have attendants to do all his works. But he will be far from being comfortable. The thinner the membrane that separates a person from the state of ultimate laziness gets, the more active the person would be. The President of United States or the richest man in the world may perhaps be the most active person on this planet.

In chemistry, when one observes electronic configuration of elements, one notices that mono-valiant elements have electronic configuration nearest to the electronic configuration of inert gases. Inert gases are the laziest substances on the earth. But the mono-valiant elements like sodium, potassium, fluorine, chlorine etc are the most active substances and it is rare to find them in pure form in nature. Where as gold, a substance that has an electronic configuration that is far away from that of an inert gas never aspires to become inert or lazy and is always genuinely lazy like the youth sleeping under the tree. Even a tri-acid mixture fails to react with gold. The persons who are far from the state of laziness are really lazy.

Coming to economics of wants and means, one finds that if the gap between wants and means is narrow, the economic entity will be very active economically. He tries to earn more. In case there is no gap between present wants and present means the economic entity, like an inert gas, will be lazy. Such a situation is, fortunately, very rare otherwise every one would have become lazy. It is truly against the will of the God. If the gap is wider, the economic entity will be lazy again like gold. Generally Government servants in countries like India fall in this category. One may notice that the developed countries like US and European countries are very active. The gap between wants and means is narrow in case of these developed countries. In case of underdeveloped countries the gap between wants and means is wider and hence they are less active economically.

Deficit budget or raising loans narrows down the gap between wants and means and this makes the countries more active. Hence I advocate deficit budget. By deficit budget you convert future means into present means. This narrows the gap between present wants and present means and the country becomes active economically. In this process latent forms of wealth like raw material, natural sources, unemployed youth etc are brought to fore and are more gainfully employed. The latent man- power that is the unemployed youth plays an important role here. I advocate the country or nation should resort to deficit budgeting as long as large manpower and resources are under-utilized.

NOTES:-

Utility Complex is a part of human brain or the brain of the economic entity (Family or Association or Company or Business Enterprise or Firm or an Organization or a State or a Nation) where wants and means are accounted and dealt with. Like water containing H+ and OH − ions, the Utility Complex is made up of wants and means. Wants and means are charged with opposite charges. Like all like charges repel each other, one want repels other want. One kind of means repel other means. There is attraction between wants and means. Means are mobile and liquid where as wants are less mobile. Because utility is made up of two components: wants and means of different charge, utility exhibit both adhesive and cohesive properties. Utility is the cementing material for various forms of wealth.

CHAPTER VIII
TIME, A FORM OF WEALTH

Often people speak of value of time. Some say that time is a precious wealth. Management accountants, while explaining the concept of Internal Rate of Return, describe the concept "Time value of Money ." Is time a form of wealth? If so, can this be proved scientifically? An attempt is made here to prove this hypothesis using known laws of science.

Coming to the definition of wealth, one can say that wealth is one that should have units and the one that can be changed to other forms of wealth. In this pretext, let us examine whether time fulfils the conditions to qualify as wealth.

Time is measurable. There are units of measurement in place for time. This fulfills the first condition. Can time be changed to other forms of wealth? Yes. Time can be changed into other forms of wealth like rent, interest etc. Does time have utility or is it soluble in the form of wealth called utility? Yes. Time is a human need. Time has utility. So going by the requirements of wealth, time amply fulfills them.

Initiating the discussion on Wants and Means, let us observe the impact when means and wants are unequal. When wants are more and means are few, any of the following measures will be undertaken by the economic entity to ensure equilibrium. When wants are more and means are few, the economic entity may adopt any or all of the following:

(1) Cheaper wants substitute costlier wants:

(2) Present wants may be changed to future wants:

(3) Future means may be cashed or future means may be changed to present means: Loans and credit purchase are the examples of conversion of future means into present means. One would be repaying these loans or credit purchase from future means.

Similarly when wants are few and means are more, the economic entity may adopt any or all of the following:

(1) Costlier wants substitute cheaper wants:

(2) Future wants may be changed to present wants: Wants that are not of immediate use may be bought or satisfied.

(3) Present means may be changed to future means by depositing money in banks in the form of term deposits or purchasing assets of use in the long term etc.

Wants and means are forms of wealth and hence one must remember that they are neither created nor are they destroyed but are changed from one form to another.

From the above discussion, it is clear that time is related to wealth. Is time a form of wealth? Does time fulfill following conditions to classify for wealth.

(1) Can time be expressed in units? Yes. Time has units of measurement.

(2) Can time be changed to other forms of wealth? Yes. Examine the following equations: Face value of deposit + time = Maturity value of deposit (Call it equation A) and Face value of deposit + Interest = maturity value of deposit (Call it equation B). Consider the equations: a + b =d and a + c = d we say that b = c. From the above equations, it is clear that value of time = interest. Mathematically, one can understand that wealth in the form of time has changed to wealth in the form of interest. The value of time may be positive as at times of inflation or may be negative as at times of deflation. At times when values of wealth are appreciated, value of time is positive and when values of wealth are depreciated, value of time is negative.

(3) Can time move from higher concentration to lower concentration like all other forms of wealth till equilibrium is reached? Yes. Examine the following:

One Year	Two Years
Rs.100 Return	Rs.100 Return
Investment A	*Investment* B

In investment B time is more concentrated as two years > one year. Therefore people tend to invest in Investment A than in Investment B. Thus one can easily see that time also moves from higher concentration to lower concentration.

Another important property of most forms of wealth is that they are soluble in this form of wealth called utility. I have used extended meaning of utility. Utility here means all that a human being/mankind needs. Is time soluble in utility? Yes. When time is soluble in utility, it undergoes economic reaction and is converted into other forms of wealth say, interest.

The concept of time as a form of wealth leads one to take first step towards classifying wealth. Wealth can be broadly classified into four classes: (1) Current means, (2) Current wants, (3) Future means (4) Future wants. Wants here mean and include all goods and services that a human being or group of human beings wants to posses. Means mean and include all forms of wealth expressed in units of money. This is in line with classification of assets and liabilities by accountants. Accountants classify assets into current assets and fixed assets.

Similarly, they classify liabilities into current liabilities and term or time liabilities. This concept of time as a form of wealth eliminates the popular concepts "Creation of wealth" and "destruction of wealth ." When money is deposited in, say, a bank, one should construe the interest earned as wealth created. Wealth in the form of time has changed into wealth in the form of interest. The deficit budget or fiscal deficit is a mode of transferring future means to current means.

When a commodity is needed for immediate use, people pay higher price to acquire the same. The value of time = value of future means – value of current means OR value of current wants – value of future wants. At times of inflation, value of current wants will be more than that of future wants. At times of inflation, value of future means will be more than value of current means. At times of inflation, value of time is positive. Similarly, at times of deflation, future value of wants will be less than present value of wants OR present value of means will be more than future value of means. In such cases value of time will be negative.

Discounted Cash Flow Technique

In evaluating the viability of a project or a venture, discounted cash flow technique is used to arrive at conclusions by people of management or financial experts. When a man is investing money in a project the out flow or costs are incurred at present and the returns or inflow or benefits are received in future. To nullify the effect of time, one has to evaluate costs and benefits at their current values.

A man, while investing in a project, is concerned about A) *Return* and B) *Risk* factors. It would be his prime objective to lessen the risks and maximize the returns. He weighs the return on this investment with alternate opportunity that involves low risk. The yield on the project should outweigh the return from any alternate source of investment that involves low risks.

The fixed costs are incurred at the start of the project. The recurring costs are incurred when project starts functioning. There may be a gap of time for returns to flow in. The costs and returns are to be compared at present value of means (both cost and return are expressed in units of money and hence are forms of means). What one spends now is worth more than what he receives at a future date. In the earlier paragraph, we have come to know that interest is one form of wealth the time changes into. To evaluate a project, costs and benefits are reduced or discounted to current values of means. At different rates of interest, costs and benefits are discounted to arrive at current worth of costs and benefits. While doing so one arrives at a rate of interest at which current worth of costs equals current worth of benefits. This rate of interest is called Internal Rate of Return. The discounting factor is arrived at using the formula;

$1 \div (1 + r/100)^n$

Here, r is the rate of interest and n is the time or number of years. This Discounted Cash Flow technique helps us evaluate a Project to arrive at economic feasibility.

When value of goods is expected to rise due to natural calamities or otherwise, people purchase the commodity in bulk and hoard. When future goods are costlier than present goods, people hoard or buy in bulk and store. When future money is expected to be dearer, people save money for future use. When present money is more valuable than future money people avail loans or cash their long-term investments like Fixed Deposits in Banks and meet their present need of money.

NOTES:-

Time meets the parameters required for consideration as wealth. Time has units of measurement. Time can be changed to other forms of wealth like interest. Time is soluble in utility or time is a human need. Time helps us classify wealth. Value of time is positive at times of inflation. Value of time is negative at times of deflation. The value of time is more clearly brought out in the Management concept called Time Value of Money. The discounted cash flow technique helps us determine value of time.

CHAPTER IX

CLASSIFICATION OF WEALTH

Generally scientists classify matter, living or otherwise, into various classes with a purpose to simplify the study of these things. An attempt is made here to evolve a scientific method of classifying wealth so as to help economists and accountants in particular and others in general to understand the general properties of each class of wealth. Can there be a foolproof method of classification? This chapter attempts to examine one method of classification of wealth with a purpose of seeking general consensus.

Chemists classify matter into three broad categories. They are elements, compounds and mixtures. Elements are substances that are made up from one or single kind of atoms. Examples for elements are: gold, silver, iron, copper etc. Compounds consist of two or more elements. The uniqueness of compounds is that the elements in the compound do not exhibit their individual properties. This can be illustrated when one studies water. Water is made up of two atoms of hydrogen and one atom of oxygen. Oxygen helps combustion and hydrogen is combustible where as water prevents combustion.

Generally, things are classified into living and non-living things. There are two broad charges of electricity: positive and negative. Similarly male and female are the two forms of advanced life. Similarly wealth can be classified into two broad categories. WANTS and MEANS are the two broad classes of wealth. Wants are the goods and services that an economic entity wants to posses or attain. Means are the money and money related forms of wealth that the economic entity uses to acquire the wants.

Wants

1. Wants comprise of goods and services that an economic entity wants to posses or acquire.

2. Wants attract means and wants repel wants

3. Wants are less mobile and one may say that they are like positively charged particles, e.g. protons.

Means

1. Means are the money and money related forms of wealth that are needed to satisfy wants.

2. Means attract wants and means repel means

3. Means are highly mobile and are liquid. We may assign them negative charge because like negatively charged electrons they are also highly mobile. One can transfer means or wealth in the form of money and money related forms from one corner of the world to the other without much difficulty.

| 4. Wants are expressed or measured in units of wealth they represent. | 4. Means are measured or expressed in units of money. Examples are: Rent, wages, salary, interest, profits, returns, loans, deposits, investments etc. |

Now, we have arrived at first step in classification of wealth. Wealth can be broadly classified into Wants (Consisting of goods and services) and Means (comprising of money and money related forms of wealth). We can write as follows;

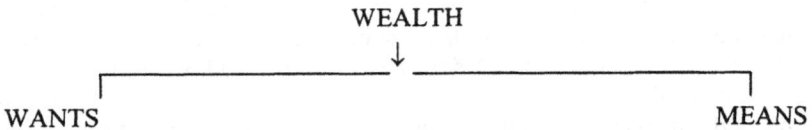

WEALTH
↓

WANTS   MEANS

After classifying wealth into two major classes WANTS and MEANS further classification should be thought of. Law of Conservation gives us the next clue for classification of wealth. In any text book of Economics one reads that wants are many and means are few. Any economic entity wants to equate "Wants" and "Means". This is because of operation of Law of Conservation of Wealth. One must have studied Law of Conservation of Mass and Law of Conservation of Energy. When matter/energy is changed from one form to another, the mass/quantity of energy of transferor and transferee form remains same and that matter/energy can neither be destroyed nor be created but can be changed from one form to another. The basic principle underlying Double Entry Bookkeeping method of Accounting is same as above. Wealth can neither be created nor be destroyed but can be changed from one form to another. Debits and credits should be equal and that assets should match liabilities. Entire Economics rests on this Law of Conservation. Every one wants a state of economy where value of Wants = value of Means.

What happens when wants are more and means are few? Wants are forms of wealth and hence cannot be destroyed. In such a situation any or all of the following may take place.

1. The economic entity may substitute costlier wants by cheaper wants. In other words wealth changes from costlier wants to cheaper wants.
2. Or alternatively, the economic entity may postpone buying or acquiring some wants. Here present wants are changed to future wants. This leads us to next class of wealth called FUTURE WANTS.
3. The economic entity may also think of availing loans or credits, which are repaid from future means.
4. Similarly, when one has more means and less wants, one notices any or all of the following:
5. Future wants may be changed to present wants i.e. the economic entity may keep stock of goods that are needed in future.
6. Costlier wants may substitute cheaper wants.

7. The economic entity may set aside some means for future use. In other
    words these are *FUTURE MEANS*. The economic entity may lend loans
    to others the repayment of which is done in future. The economic entity
    may deposit money in banks or purchase shares or debentures. All these
    are FUTRE MEANS. Present means are converted into future means. We
    have now arrived at second subdivision of wealth: *A) Current
    Means/Wants and B) Future Means/Wants*.

Loans, credits, advances, investments etc are future means. Current
deposits, current holdings etc. are Present means. Wages are means and labor
is a want. One's wants are other's means.

In short, wealth can be broadly divided into two classes namely Wants
and Means. These wants and means can be further subdivided into four sub-
classes: Present Wants, Future Wants, Present Means and Future Means. We
may classify wants into A) goods and B) services. Further classification may
be arrived at in many ways: we may consider goods and services that satisfy
physical needs, goods and services that are used to manufacture other goods
etc. We may consider classifying goods and services in the manner chemists
classify matter. One may term the wealth that consists of only one form of
wealth as elemental wealth e.g. gold, food etc. OR one may call such wealth,
which satisfies single utility, as elemental wealth. Raw materials may be
classified as elemental wealth and finished goods as compound wealth. In
finished goods, we find different forms of wealth like raw material, power and
labor. Alternatively, goods that satisfy physical need like food, shelter etc
may be grouped in one family. OR we may classify goods into essential
goods, luxury goods etc. Means can be further subdivided based on their
liquidity. Means like cash have highest liquidity and means like shares have
low liquidity.

We may denote wealth by using symbols the way elements are denoted.
Chemists denote Oxygen by O and Hydrogen by H. We may use M for
money, I for investments, R for rent, C for capital etc. We may use existing
notations in cases of some forms of wealth. We may classify wealth in the
form of food into following sub-classes like oils, pulses, cereals, sugars etc.
This is just a beginning and lot of work is to be done.

CHAPTER X
MATTER, ENERGY, WEALTH AND SOUL

Matter, energy, wealth and soul are the forms the God almighty exhibits. Law of Conservation and Law of Equilibrium are His two important Laws or rather His two characteristics. It is no wonder that matter, energy, wealth and soul also exhibit the two characters. Law of Conservation: Matter/energy/wealth/soul can neither be created nor be destroyed but can be changed from one form to another. Matter can be changed from one form to another and so are energy and wealth. . In Bhagavad-Gita Lord Krishna says" Sword cannot cut the Soul, Water cannot wet the soul and Fire cannot burn the soul. Soul is immortal. Soul changes bodies the way we change our clothes." This is in simple words Law of Conservation of Soul. If one goes by the understanding that God cannot be created nor can he be destroyed as stated in various religious books Law of Conservation can be stated as one of His characteristics or properties. Law of Equilibrium ensures Law of Conservation. Matter/energy/wealth/soul moves from higher concentration/level to lower concentration/level till the concentration/level at both ends equalize or in other words till equilibrium is reached.

Matter, energy, wealth and soul are interlinked. When matter or an atom is broken in a nuclear reactor enormous energy is released. Wealth is made up of matter, energy and soul (human element). Wealth is inseparable from matter, energy and soul. Matter, wealth, energy and soul are inter-convertible. When food is consumed and assimilated, energy is released. Energy contained in the matter is released. This energy is made use of by the soul. This results in uplifting soul. Wealth in the form of food when consumed by soul, results in increase in the value of soul as a form of wealth. This should form an interesting topic for researchers, as lot has to be unearthed. This study should lead us to understanding the God and His creation. It will be good news if this Law of Conservation is true that the living world and the world of resources never see an end. There will be life and there will be resources of energy and matter for millions of years to come. There is no need to panic. Let us consider the relation between matter and wealth. More the quantity of matter more will be the (value of) wealth. There exists a direct relationship between matter (or mass) and wealth. Similarly there is a direct relationship between energy and wealth. More the energy contained in a fuel more its value is in terms of wealth. Rich sources of energy like uranium, radium etc has very high value as wealth. More the number of souls more will be the quantity of wealth. Some economists or demographists state that India shall be a major power, economically, and politically, in 2020's considering the human resource that she (India is always written in female gender) will have then. So there exists a direct relation between soul and wealth.

Matter, energy and wealth are directly related to soul or the human being. The essence of wealth "Value in USE" is the measure of importance of matter, or energy or wealth to the human being or mankind in the larger perspective. Matter and energy should be of use to mankind or soul to qualify for wealth. In this universe there is no substance that is useless to mankind or soul. Even poison has value in use. Disease causing bacteria have value in use. They help maintain eco-balance. It is not true that all that have more value in use have more value in exchange or price. Substances like water, air and food have very high value in use but have very little value in exchange. God has assured justice in a way that all can have access to these important requirements of life at affordable cost or price or effort.

Soul or human being spends money or wealth for acquiring knowledge. Companies spend money for up gradation of skills of their workers. They spend money on training needs of their employees. Money is spent here on knowledge or wealth in the form of money is changed to wealth in the form of knowledge here. This leads to important conclusion that knowledge is wealth. When soul or human being receives knowledge his value in exchange increases. Knowledge is an integral part of the soul and it enhances value of soul.

The soul or human being forms the center of all economic activity. The utility of matter and energy to the soul or the human being forms the very core or substance of wealth. It is time now to study the general properties matter, energy, wealth and soul.

Common properties of Matter, energy and Wealth:

Law of conservation is applicable to all three.

 (1) Matter/energy/wealth can neither be created nor be destroyed but can be changed one form to another.

 (2) Law of Equilibrium applies to all three. Matter moves from higher level/concentration to lower concentration. E.g. when a tire of a vehicle is burst, air moves out of the tire as tire contains air stored at high pressure. When one mixes hot water with cold water, heat moves from higher temperature to lower temperature. Wealth also moves from higher concentration to lower concentration.

 (3) Matter, energy and wealth are measurable. Wealth generally acquires units of matter and energy for measurement. When wealth in the form of a vegetable, say potato is to be measured units of measurement of potato or in other words units of measurement of weight are used. When wealth in the forms of *Means* is being measured, units of money are used.

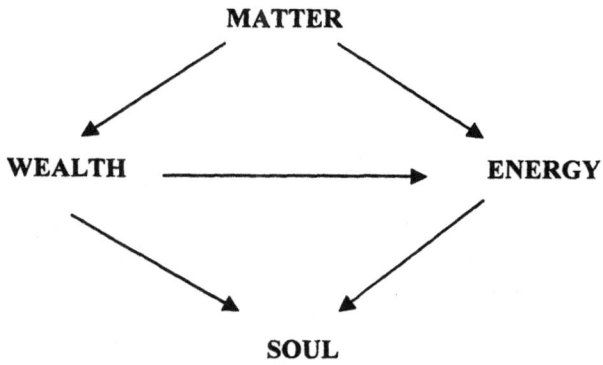

CHAPTER XI
SUMMARY

Wealth, like matter, energy and soul is a manifestation of the God. Wealth is measurable. Wealth has units of measurement. Wealth can neither be created nor can be destroyed but can be changed from one form to another. Wealth, like matter and energy, moves from higher concentration to lower concentration till equilibrium is reached.

Law of Conservation of Wealth and Law of Equilibrium are the two General Laws of Wealth. These laws are faces of a same coin. They always operate together. Law of Mass Action, a law meant for chemical reactions, applies to all economic reactions where wealth changes from one form to another. All economic reactions are reversible and this is the reason why there ought to be a credit of like amount for every debit in bookkeeping.

The Law of Mass Action of chemistry is a general law for all reactions of change of wealth from one form to another. According to this law the rate of any economic reaction is directly proportional to the quantity of reacting substances. If quantity of one form of wealth increases, its relative value in terms of other form/s of wealth decreases. When commodities increase their relative value in money terms decreases. If houses increase, their value in terms of rent decreases. If commodities increase their relative value in utility terms decreases or marginal utility decreases..

Wealth may or may not have value in exchange. Loss, depreciation and goodwill are some examples of forms of wealth that may/may not have value in exchange. It is a common notion that when a form/forms of wealth, which have value in use, are changed into form/s of wealth that have value in exchange wealth is created. Example for this is PHOTOSYNTHESIS. Here wealth in the forms of Carbon dioxide and water (in presence of wealth in the forms of chlorophyll and sunlight), combine to form wealth in the form of food. Chlorophyll, sunlight, soil moisture, carbon dioxide and essential plant nutrients present in the soil do not have value in exchange where as wealth in the form of food has value in exchange. When wealth that has value in exchange is changed to wealth that has value in use we call that wealth is lost. All consumption and expenditure reactions belong to this category.

Time is a form of wealth. It is measurable and it can be transferred to other known forms of wealth like rent and interest. Utility, the human need, is the form of wealth in which all other forms of wealth dissolve. This utility, like water in chemistry, comprises of two distinct parts: wants, that comprise wants and goods, and means, that comprise money and money related forms of wealth. Utility exhibits both adhesive and cohesive properties. Utility binds utility and utility binds two forms of wealth the way water acts as adhesive and cohesive agent.

The concept of equivalent weight of chemistry is applicable to wealth. In a chemical reaction, forms of matter react in the ratio of equivalent weight and in an economic reaction, say sale, materials are exchanged or react with money in the ratio of price. Price, Marginal utility or utility equivalent, rate of exchange and rate of return are some words denoting concept of equivalence.

No attempt is made as on date to classify forms of wealth and to study these forms of wealth in a systematic way. Wealth can be classified broadly in two categories: wants comprising of goods and services and means comprising of money and money related forms of wealth.

There is an inseparable bonding between matter, energy, wealth and soul. Matter, energy and soul are all wealth. Matter, energy, wealth and soul can neither be created nor be destroyed but can be changed from one form to another.